SIX EXISTENTIALIST THINKERS

hαrper ✝ τorchbooks

*A reference-list of Harper Torchbooks, classified
by subjects, is printed at the end of this volume.*

SIX EXISTENTIALIST THINKERS

BY

H. J. BLACKHAM

HARPER TORCHBOOKS

THE ACADEMY LIBRARY

HARPER & ROW, PUBLISHERS

NEW YORK AND EVANSTON

SIX EXISTENTIALIST THINKERS

Reprinted by arrangement with The Macmillan Company, New York,
which published the original edition in 1952.

First HARPER TORCHBOOK edition published 1959

TB 1002

2098

60 - 280

Library of Congress catalog card number: ~~59–13840~~

PREFACE

THE purpose of this book is exposition, not criticism nor advocacy. There have been enough popular accounts of the general ideas of existentialists. It is time to discriminate between these thinkers; they are not exponents of a school, and yet not the least impressive thing about their highly individual thought, separated by age, nationality, and temperament, is the interrelatedness of their thinking: they lead into each other; they form a natural family; each throws light on the others, and together they develop the content of certain common themes. For this reason, the book should be read as a whole.

The excuse for trying to get these writers a hearing in English in summary form is that the contemporary ones are not yet fully translated and are voluminous and not easy to read. These studies may serve as an introduction and as a clue. The final essay is not intended as a critical assessment; it is still interpretative, and designed to remove some of the prevalent misunderstandings and dispose of some of the fanciful criticisms.

Although these studies appeal to the reader to take each thinker individually on his merits and not as the exponent of a school, it is permissible to try to see the movement in the grand perspective of human thought. It appears to be reaffirming in a modern idiom the protestant or the stoic form of individualism, which stands over against the empirical individualism of the Renaissance or of modern liberalism or of Epicurus as well as over against the universal system of Rome or of Moscow or of Plato. These are permanent types of thought and attitude, deeper than any formal doctrine or belief. As pure types, they show excesses and deficiencies which the various forms of compromise escape; and they show dramatic qualities which only pure forms can have. If this analysis is sound, existential-ism is not (as some think) an hysterical symptom of the irrationalism associated with the violence and disintegration of our time: it is a contemporary renewal of one of the necessary phases of human experience in a conflict of ideals which history has not yet resolved. If it has this order of importance, it is worth serious attention.

Finally, the general reader who is interested enough to want to acquaint himself with existentialism should be told at the outset that there is nothing in this book which he cannot understand if he really wants to. There are difficulties, but they are not technical, and they are likely to oppress the philosopher even more than the general reader.

H.J.B.

CONTENTS

PREFACE   *page* v

I. SØREN KIERKEGAARD   1

II. FRIEDRICH NIETZSCHE   23

III. KARL JASPERS   43

IV. GABRIEL MARCEL   66

V. MARTIN HEIDEGGER   86

VI. JEAN-PAUL SARTRE   110

VII. A PHILOSOPHY OF PERSONAL EXISTENCE   149

BIOGRAPHICAL NOTES   166

BIBLIOGRAPHICAL NOTES   169

INDEX   171

I

SØREN KIERKEGAARD

(1813-1855)

I

KIERKEGAARD pertinaciously challenged his countrymen on their pretensions to Christian faith and made the vanity of their German culture the constant target of his Attic wit. The seriousness of his sustained campaign sealed his separation from normal domestic happiness and from the fellowship of his generation, condemned him to loneliness and a tragic role. 'Like a solitary fir tree egoistically separate and pointed upward I stand, casting no shadow, and only the wood-dove builds its nest in my branches.' Whether his was a case of the prophet without honour in his own country, or just a case, is a difference of opinion between his many disciples and admirers in the world to-day and others who having neither sympathy nor patience either with him or with his ideas explain both from the sufficient evidence of his neurosis and its cause. At least the disciples have read and studied him, and it is safe to say that nobody can read him to any extent without being permanently impressed by the exceptional intellectual and literary power of the man and the genuine totality of his Christian inwardness. He was physically deformed, he was crippled by a sense of guilt, he was 'a genius in a market town': this was a mixture that had to explode in excess, an extreme concentration or an extreme dissipation. The absolute disjunction of his first book *Either-Or*, which remained the clue to all his thinking, was not merely nor mainly the slogan of his attack upon the Hegelian

1

principle of mediation and synthesis, but was rooted, and consciously rooted, in his personal need for tension, passion, sacrifice, individuality. Between the absolute of concentration and of dissipation the choice was inevitably certain: he proposed to think and will one thing, and became a man set apart, a sacrifice, a personality, whose challenge to his time was carefully planned and copiously and energetically worked out to a conclusion in his active life, with effects that still reverberate in theology and philosophy; whilst in his inner orientation he became a man turned away from this world 'who historically speaking died of a mortal disease, but poetically speaking died of longing for eternity'.

Philosophical Fragments[1] (1844) and *Concluding Unscientific Post-script*[2] (1846) are the central works in the development of Kierkegaard's life-purpose. Together, the two books present as directly and methodically as can be expected the philosophical thinking of a man whose method is indirect and whose philosophy is not a system. The titles are in themselves characteristic hits at the elaborate system established under the rule of Hegel ('the System'). Existentialism begins as a voice raised in protest against the absurdity of Pure Thought, a logic which is not the logic of thinking but the immanent movements of Being. It recalls the spectator of all time and of all existence from the speculations of Pure Thought to the problems and the possibilities of his own conditioned thinking as an existing individual seeking to know how to live and to live the life he knows. Kierkegaard imagines how Socrates would tease Hegel, with dialectical skill interrupting his flights and keeping him down to earth. His strength against Hegel at this time of the tremendous swell and boom of Hegel's reputation on the Continent derives from the sharp pangs of his own need for something to live by. In his student days, having rejected Christianity, he devoted himself to Hegel.

'Let a doubting youth, an existing doubter, imbued with a lovable and unlimited youthful confidence in a hero of thought, confidingly seek in Hegel's positive philosophy the truth, the truth for existence: he will write a formidable epigram over Hegel . . . let him submit himself unconditionally, in feminine devotion, but with sufficient vigour of determination to hold fast to his problem: he will become a

[1] Translated by David F. Swenson. Princeton, 1936.
[2] Translated by David F. Swenson and Walter Lowrie. Princeton, 1941.

satirist without suspecting it. The youth is an existing doubter. Hovering in doubt and without a foothold for his life, he reaches out for the truth—in order to exist in it. He is negative and the philosophy of Hegel is positive—what wonder then that he seeks anchorage in Hegel. But a philosophy of pure thought is for an existing individual a chimera, if the truth that is sought is something to exist in. To exist under the guidance of pure thought is like travelling in Denmark with the help of a small map of Europe, on which Denmark shows no larger than a steel pen-point—aye, it is still more impossible. The admiration and enthusiasm of the youth, his boundless confidence in Hegel, is precisely the satire upon Hegel.' (*Concluding Unscientific Postscript*, p. 275.)

The disillusionment with speculative philosophy and his continuing despair sent him back to the question of Christian faith and founded his settled hostility to objective system-building as a distraction and a delusion, ruinous to truly philosophical thinking and living because it provides a life-long escape from the real problems of individual existence.

In rejecting Christianity, Kierkegaard had perceived the discontinuity between faith and reason, and in rejecting speculative philosophy he retained this perception and built his position upon it. He made it the effort of his life to renew the meaning of Christianity by compelling recognition of the permanent cleavage between faith and reason, Christianity and culture. Whereas the Christian revelation had been naturalized, assimilated, made probable and acceptable, an inheritance, reconciled with the rest of history in a total world view, there could be no genuine Christianity that was not an irremediable absurdity, a perpetual offence, posing a choice, a fateful decision. Here there reappears a persistent tendency in Christian thought. Always there is the attempt to reconcile faith and reason, to philosophize Christian beliefs, to graft revelation into the tree of natural theology—to be plainly seen in such different systems as those of St. Thomas Aquinas, Ficino, or Hegel. Sooner or later comes the extrusion of Christian beliefs as wholly alien to reason and experience, incapable of assimilation, a limit and a challenge to thought—the work in their different ways of a Pomponazzi, a Luther, a Pascal, a Kierkegaard. Such a movement of thought may spring from the tension between a sceptical mind and a religious heart, but it represents also the persistent tension between Christian dogma and secular culture.

3

Kierkegaard's argument deals with the object of Christian faith and the manner of apprehending it. That a man born and living in history says that he is God and dies in humiliation plunges into a dilemma those who would build their lives on him and his word. Nothing has happened since to lighten by one scruple the strain on belief. The historical success of Christianity is worthless evidence. The present generation is exactly in the position of the contemporaries of Christ who witnessed his humiliation on the cross. Faith to-day, unless it is faith in the faith of the Apostles, is not other than their faith in the man who makes the most absurd of claims. The truth of this claim cannot in the nature of the case be made objectively certain, or even investigated: on the contrary, the absolute discontinuity between the human and the divine which inheres in the conception of God makes it unthinkable, so that it cannot by any human mind be recognized as true, cannot be entertained as a possibility. The perception of a truth (in geometry, for example) through the mediation of a teacher is a process of learning which cannot apply to the object of religious faith. If the active reason eagerly accepts the truth of the Incarnation, it is merely deceived; for it claims to be able to recognize the inconceivable in the familiar. No possible education can make reason capable of this attainment. If a man claims to be God, then, all that reason can do is to take notice of this claim and give special attention to all the circumstances attending it. Inquiry into the authenticity of the evidence (itself never finally conclusive) is beside the point, however, for if the historical facts were established beyond cavil the inquirer would be no nearer to making up his mind what to make of them. The Incarnation is a paradox which can never be thought nor accepted by reason, and therefore the claim that it is the supreme truth imposes a limit on thought and throws the inquirer into a passion of uncertainty. If, by the grace of God, he sets reason and experience aside and joins himself to the paradox in the passion of faith, he is 'out upon the deep, over seventy thousand fathoms of water' and risks everything. The decision to take the risk cannot bring certainty. The unintelligibility of the paradox remains absolute, incapable of being reduced or got round. Its acceptance by faith does nothing to reduce its offence to reason: it is in perpetual tension with the intelligence, a cause of suffering and passion, reducing the most powerful understanding to the level of the most simple, and both to nothing; for it poses itself as the limit of all thought, and the question at issue is eternal happiness.

4

The decision of faith entails an ethical decision to renounce the world, to break off all attachments, especially the most cherished. No more than the decision of faith can this be externalized and made once for all (by retirement to a monastery, for example). The believer goes on as before with no perceptible external difference, but the internal difference is total. Everything is resigned; at the same time all that was formerly enjoyed is still actually possessed and the desire for it is therefore accentuated: resignation, possession, desire are equally real and daily renewed. This maintains an inner tension of suffering and passion which increases the tension of faith and reason. As a classical instance of the break between normal human life and the life of faith, is the case of Abraham's readiness to sacrifice Isaac, in which the most sacred ethical certainty of human living is given up to the uncertainty of faith, something profoundly abhorrent and cruelly wounding to the self and utterly condemned by reason is done with the decision but not the certainty that it is right.

Such is Christianity, an intrusion into the life of reason, a disruption of society, an established Christian society most of all. Its challenge to human thinking and willing is permanently disconcerting, for it is a voice which speaks to man's condition but one which he can never hear with his own ears.

Kierkegaard's theology is the revivalist's call to repentance: conviction of sin, despair, repentance and conversion, turning to Christ for salvation, the gift of faith, new birth and the life of grace. Sophisticated Christians are accused of adulterous dalliance with philosophy and invited to recognize that to become a Christian means humiliating faithfulness to this uncouth fundamentalism. To grow up in the proud inheritance of a Christian civilization is to be disastrously oblivious of the fundamental thing, as though a generation of Venetians should fail to notice that their city is built upon piles. A Christian civilization is nothing other than the quantity of individual souls living by personal decision on the Christian faith. This invisible quantitative reality produces visible results. 'It is the quantitative that gives to life its manifold variety, ever weaving its motley tapestry; it is that sister of Destiny who sat spinning at the wheel. But Thought is the other sister, whose task it is to cut the thread; which, leaving the figure, should be done every time the quantitative attempts to create a new quality.' Here is Kierkegaard the Thinker challenging Hegel and modern sophistication, like Elijah on Mount Carmel casting back to the living primitive faith of the desert, refusing the destiny of union with the superior culture of Canaan—a fateful decision.[1] The importance of Kierkegaard is that he is the thinker and not merely the preacher. He is both, one and indivisible: he is Elijah and Socrates. 'My whole life is an epigram calculated to make people aware.' In that sentence from his Journal, he sums up his conscious mission. His whole life is his teaching, not merely his writings, and it is an epigram, the extreme of concentration and renunciation (to think and will one thing); it is calculated, deliberately and elaborately planned; and the teaching does not pretend to engender anything, but only to help to bring forth. As a personality, as wholly dedicated to the midwife's art, as a master (one of the very greatest) of irony, he plays the Socratic part in modern philosophy, seeking to make his contemporaries aware of their flight from themselves and their secret despair, and of what it means to be an existing individual and what it means to become a Christian. He is a prophet denouncing a generation which had sold its birthright of inquisitive ignorance for a mass of information. He is a philosopher as well as a Christian fundamentalist, Denmark's foremost philosopher, concerned with the fundamental validities of thought and will, and rejecting speculative philosophy not only because it patronized the Christian faith but also because it confused the categories, subordinating ethical will to disinterested intelligence in a false and fatal hierarchy, substituting illusory visions for vital decisions.

II

The critical philosophy of Kant answers the primary question of modern philosophy (what can I know?) in a way which challenges all and satisfies none. If thought forms its object by arranging and interpreting appearances according to principles shared by all minds as such in their common constitution, and can never know the thing-in-itself which is the ground of appearances, the inter-subjectivity of established science is accounted for, but its value as knowledge

[1] Hegel in his early historical studies picked on Abraham's separation of himself from his native country and his kindred, a drastic cutting loose from natural ties and cultural roots, as producing at the outset the defining essence of Judaism. The essence is reproduced in S.K. himself. See Nohl, *Hegels theologische Jugendschriften*, p. 243 *seq.*; p. 371 *seq.*

of reality is equivocal and the road is open to scepticism and nihilism. Hegel, in the most audacious and ambitious effort of modern philosophy to establish the unity of thought and Béing, tried to show that thought is able to think its object because all nature and all history are in themselves the means by which thought becomes an object to itself—just as I know myself by what I have become. The structure of thought and things is homogeneous throughout. His prodigious demonstration of this thesis showed Kierkegaard not that the rational is the real but that pure thought is pure fantasy. Thought and things are not homogeneous. Thought in abstracting from existence in a philosophy of history is dealing with itself not with existence; the actualities of becoming which make the real process and cannot be thought are lost sight of and escape, leaving the thinker with his illusion. Hegel, therefore, does not do better than Kant.

'A scepticism which attacks thought itself cannot be vanquished by thinking it through, since the very instrument by which this would have to be done is in revolt. There is only one thing to do with such a scepticism, and that is to break with it. To answer Kant within the fantastic shadow-play of pure thought is precisely not to answer him. The only thing-in-itself which cannot be thought is existence, and this does not come within the province of thought to think . . . .

'Instead of conceding the contention of Idealism, but in such a manner as to dismiss as a temptation the entire problem of a reality in the sense of a thing-in-itself eluding thought, which like other temptations cannot be vanquished by giving way to it; instead of putting an end to Kant's misleading reflection which brings reality into connexion with thought; instead of relegating reality to the ethical—Hegel scored a veritable advance; for he became fantastic and vanquished idealistic scepticism by means of pure thought, which is merely an hypothesis, and even if it does not so declare itself, a fantastic hypothesis. The triumphant victory of pure thought, that in it being and thought are one, is something both to laugh at and to weep over, since in the realm of pure thought it is not even possible to distinguish them. That thought has validity was assumed by Greek philosophy without question. By reflecting over the matter one would have to arrive at the same result; but why confuse the validity of thought with reality? A valid thought is a possibility, and every further question as to whether it is real or not should be dismissed as irrelevant.' (*Concluding Unscientific Postscript*, p. 292.)

Thought, then, is ideal, pure intelligibility, possibility, and therefore other than existence. How is it related to the existence which it cannot think? It is the existing individual who thinks—intermittently. He thinks before and after, and his thought is relevant to and valid for his existence. Thus the prime and proper business of thought is with the thinker's personal existence, since he is related to every other reality as to a possibility. It is a misunderstanding to be concerned about any reality other than one's own ethical reality: each individual is isolated and compelled to exist for himself. The individual cannot be defined; he can be known only by himself from within. His own being is the first and proper object of his thinking, by which he is to judge of everything else. 'Socrates was a man whose energies were devoted to thinking; but he reduced all other knowledge to indifference in that he infinitely accentuated ethical knowledge.'

'To assert the supremacy of thought is Gnosticism; to make the ethical reality of the subject the only reality might seem to be acosmism. The circumstance that it will seem so to a busy thinker who explains everything, a nimble mind that quickly surveys the entire universe, merely proves that such a thinker has a very humble notion of what the ethical means to the subject. If Ethics were to take away the entire world from such a thinker, letting him keep his own self, he would probably regard such a trifle as not worth keeping, and would let it go with the rest—and so it becomes acosmism. But why does he think so slightingly of his own self? If it were our meaning that he should give up the whole world in order to content himself with another person's ethical reality, he would be justified in regarding the exchange as a dead loss. But his own ethical reality, on the other hand, ought to mean more to him than "heaven and earth and all that therein is", more than the six thousand years of human history, more than both astrology and the veterinary sciences or whatever it is that the age demands, all of which is aesthetically and intellectually a huge vulgarity. And if it is not so, it is worse for the individual himself, for in that case he has absolutely nothing, no reality at all, since to all other things the maximum relationship attainable is possibility.' (Ibid., p. 305.)

What is meant by this ethical reality of the subject? Since existence consists in movement, 'the difficulty facing an existing individual is how to give his existence the continuity without which everything simply vanishes'. The answer is: 'The goal of movement for an existing individual is to arrive at a decision, and to renew it'. The thinker gives himself stable ethical reality by forming and renewing himself in critical decisions which are a total inward commitment (decisions, for example, as to vocation, marriage, faith). 'Through having willed in this manner, through having ventured to take a decisive step in the utmost intensity of subjective passion and with full consciousness of one's eternal responsibility (which is within the capacity of every human being), one learns something else about life, and learns that it is quite a different thing from being engaged, year in and year out, in piecing together something for a system.'

'This ethical reality is the only reality which does not become a mere possibility through being known, and which can be known only through being thought; for it is the individual's own reality. Before it became a reality it was known by him in the form of a conceived reality, and hence as a possibility. But in the case of another person's reality he could have no knowledge about it until he conceived it in coming to know it, which means that he transformed it from a reality into a possibility . . . .

'When I think something which I propose to do but have not yet done, the content of this conception, no matter how exact it may be, if it be ever so much entitled to be called a conceived reality, is a possibility. Conversely, when I think about something that another has done, and so conceive a reality, I lift this given reality out of the real and set it into the possible; for a conceived reality is a possibility, and is higher than reality from the standpoint of thought, but not from the standpoint of reality. This implies that there is no immediate relationship, ethically, between subject and subject. When I understand another person, his reality is for me a possibility, and in its aspect of possibility this conceived reality is related to me precisely as the thought of something I have not done is related to the doing of it.' (Ibid., pp. 284, 285.)

Even historical reality is apprehended as possibility, and even its decisive ethical influence on conduct is independent of the question as to its actuality.

'It is everlastingly untrue that anyone was ever helped to do the good by the fact that someone else really did it; for if he ever comes to the point of really doing it himself, it will be by apprehending the reality of the other as a possibility. When Themistocles was rendered sleepless by thinking about the exploits of Miltiades, it was his apprehension of their reality as a possibility that made him sleepless. Had he plunged into inquiries as to whether Miltiades really had accomplished the great things attributed to him, had he contented himself with knowing that Miltiades had actually done them, he would scarcely have been rendered sleepless. In that case he would probably have become a sleepy, or at the most a noisy admirer, but scarcely a second Miltiades. Ethically speaking there is nothing so conducive to sound sleep as admiration of another person's ethical reality. And again ethically speaking, if there is anything that can stir and rouse a man, it is a possibility ideally requiring itself of a human being.' (Ibid., p. 321.)

The only way to avoid confusion, error, and misdirection of effort is to hold separate in their appropriate spheres the intellectual and the aesthetic, the ethical and the religious; and to give them their unity where it is properly found, in the life of the existing individual under the supremacy of the ethical, not in the abstraction of pure thought under the supremacy of the intellectual. 'Ethics concentrates upon the individual, and ethically it is the task of every individual to become an entire man; just as it is the ethical presupposition that every man is born in such a condition that he can become one.' There is a natural disposition, chronic in some ages, to escape from existence into the aesthetic and the intellectual, and to find in these preoccupations a dispensation from the decisions and experience which form and mature the personal self. One who lives in the aesthetic, plays emotionally and imaginatively with all possibilities, renounces nothing, commits himself as little as possible in vocation, marriage, belief, enjoys a literary interest in all faiths and customs and relationships, comes and goes in his wishes and desires of the moment, and is subject to fortune and misfortune. One who lives in the intellectual, claims to rise above the world of change and chance, to regard and judge everything from the point of view of the eternal, with detachment, to put everything in its place in the system, co-ordinated and understood. 'One does not live any more, one does not act, one does not believe; but one knows what love and faith are, and it only remains to determine their place in the System.'

'Science organizes the moments of subjectivity within a knowledge of them, and this knowledge is assumed to be the highest stage, and all knowledge is an abstraction which annuls existence, a taking of the objects of knowledge out of existence. In existence, however, such a principle does not hold. If thought speaks deprecatingly of the imagination, imagination in its turn speaks deprecatingly of thought; and likewise with feeling. The task is not to exalt the one at the expense of the other, but to give them an equal status, to unify them in simultaneity; the medium in which they are unified is *existence*.

'By positing as a task the scientific process instead of the existential simultaneity, life is confused. Even where the succession is obvious, as in the case of the different ages in the individual's life, the task is to achieve simultaneity. It may be a genial observation that the world and the human race have grown older; but is not everyone still born in infancy? In the life of the individual the task is to achieve an ennoblement of the successive within the simultaneous. To have been young, and then to grow older, and finally to die, is a very mediocre form of human existence; this merit belongs to every animal. But the unification of the different stages of life in simultaneity is the task set for human beings. And just as it is an evidence of mediocrity when a human beings cuts away all communication with childhood, so as to be a man merely fragmentarily, so it is also a miserable mode of existence for a thinker who is also an existing individual to lose imagination and feeling, which is quite as bad as losing his reason.'

'. . . The true is not higher than the good and the beautiful, but the true and the good and the beautiful belong essentially to every human existence, and are unified for an existing individual not in thought but in existence.' (Ibid., p. 311.)

To live in the ethical is to commit oneself, to put oneself beyond fortune and misfortune by an infinite religious resignation, to cut short protracted deliberation and the endless approximation process of research in order to take the intellectual decisions necessary to live and to become something definite; and the elaboration of this something definite is the aesthetic in its right place, subordinated to the ethical in the thinker's existence in so far as he makes himself a work of art.

'. . . one would suppose that a thinker lived the richest human life—so at least it was in Greece.

It is different with the abstract thinker who without having understood himself, or the relationship that abstract thought bears to existence, simply follows the promptings of his talent or is made by training to become something of this sort. I am very well aware that one tends to admire an artistic career where the artist simply pursues his talent without at all making himself clear over what it means to be a human being, and that our admiration tends to forget the person of the artist over his artistry. But I also know that such a life has its tragedy in being a differential type of existence not personally reflected in the ethical; and I know that in Greece, at least, a thinker was not a stunted, crippled creature who produced works of art, but was himself a work of art in his existence.' (Ibid., p. 269.)

The one-sidedness of the artist or the thinker is unavoidable, but that is something to be compensated and mitigated. It even has its virtue. But when it is both misconceived and exalted and becomes the delusion of the age, it is time to show clearly exactly what is being done.

'I am well aware that every human being is more or less one-sided, and I do not regard it as a fault. But it is a fault when a fashion selects a certain form of one-sidedness and magnifies it into a total norm. *Non omnes omnia possumus* is a maxim that holds true everywhere in life; but the ideal task should not on that account be forgotten. The one-sidedness should partly be apprehended, not without a certain sadness, and partly it should represent a vigorous resolution of the will, preferring to be something definite in a manner worth while, rather than to be a dabbler in everything. Every distinguished individual always has something one-sided about him, and this one-sidedness may be an indirect indication of his real greatness, but it is not that greatness itself. So far are we human beings from realizing the ideal, that the second rank, the powerful one-sidedness, is pretty much the highest ever attained; but it must never be forgotten that it is only the second rank. It might be urged that the present generation is, from this point of view, praiseworthy, in so one-sidedly aiming to express the intellectual and the scientific. My answer would be that the misfortune of the present age is not that it is one-sided, but that it is abstractly all-sided. A one-sided individual rejects, clearly and definitely, what he does not wish to include; but the abstractly all-sided individual imagines that he has everything through the one-sidedness of the intellectual. A one-sided believer refuses to have anything to do with thought, and a one-sided man of action will have nothing to do with science; but the one-sidedness of the intellectual creates the illusion of having everything. A one-sided individual of this type has faith and passion as transcended phases of his life, or so he says—and nothing is easier to say.' (Ibid., p. 312.)

Thus a mistaken philosophy may infect a culture and distract the entire age, since human beings are ever ready to evade their proper destiny and the anxious personal decisions it entails. In such an age the existential thinker founding himself upon his own ethical reality will be out of place and will call to deaf ears, to men hiding from their own despair.

'In spite of all his exertion the subjective thinker enjoys only a meager reward. The more the collective idea comes to dominate even the ordinary consciousness, the more forbidding seems the transition to becoming a particular existing human being instead of losing oneself in the race, and saying "we, our age, the nineteenth century". That it is a little thing merely to be a particular existing human being is not to be denied; but for this very reason it requires considerable resignation not to make light of it. For what does a mere individual count for? Our age knows only too well how little it is, but here also lies the specific immorality of the age. Each age has its own characteristic depravity. Ours is perhaps not pleasure or indulgence or sensuality, but rather a dissolute pantheistic contempt for the individual man. In the midst of all our exultation over the achievements of the age and the nineteenth century, there sounds a note of poorly conceived contempt for the individual man; in the midst of the self-importance of the contemporary generation there is revealed a sense of despair over being human. Everything must attach itself so as to be a part of some movement; men are determined to lose themselves in the totality of things, in world-history, fascinated and deceived by a magic witchery; no one wants to be an individual human being. Hence perhaps the many attempts to continue to cling to Hegel, even by men who have reached an insight into the questionable character of his philosophy. It is a fear that if they were to become particular existing human beings, they would vanish tracelessly, so that not even the daily press would be able to discover them, still less critical journals, to say nothing at all of speculative

13

philosophers immersed in world-history. As particular human beings they fear that they will be doomed to a more isolated and forgotten existence than that of a man in the country; for if a man lets go of Hegel he will not even be in a position to have a letter addressed to him.' (Ibid., p. 317.)

Thus modern philosophy in its very ambition is aloof from the entire point and offers a despairing individual not edification in the life he can live, but distraction, dissipation, and destruction.

'In Greece, philosophizing was a mode of action, and the philosopher was therefore an existing individual. He may not have possessed a great amount of knowledge, but what he did know he knew to some profit, because he busied himself early and late with the same thing. But nowadays, just what is it to philosophize, and what does a philosopher really know? For of course I do not deny that he knows everything.' (Ibid., p. 295.)

A true philosophy, articulating the intellectual, the aesthetic, and the ethical in the living body of an existing individual would teach the inquirer to know and meet the requirements of his situation. Such a philosophy would also teach him to distinguish faith as a fourth category not to be confused with any of the others. For if Christianity were merely a doctrine, it could be apprehended intellectually. If Christianity were merely a teacher with a doctrine, the doctrine would be more important than the teacher and the maximum attainment would be to apprehend it intellectually with an entire indifference to the person of the teacher. If Christianity were merely the person of the teacher himself as a moral exemplar, his historical reality (like that of Miltiades) would be a matter of indifference; he would exist as he only could exist for another, in the realm of possibility. But the Christian believer is infinitely interested in the reality of another, as in his own.

'The object of faith is the reality of the teacher, that the teacher really exists. The answer of faith is therefore unconditionally yes or no. For it does not concern a doctrine, as to whether the doctrine is true or not; it is the answer to a question concerning a fact: "Do you or do you not suppose that he has really existed?" And the answer, it must be noted, is with infinite passion. In the case of a human being, it is thoughtlessness to lay so great and infinite a stress on the question whether he has existed or not. If the object of faith is a human being, therefore, the whole proposal is the vagary of a stupid person, who has not even understood the spirit of the intellectual and the aesthetic. The object of faith is hence the reality of the God-man in the sense of his existence.' (Ibid., p. 290.)

This question is to be decided by a personal decision of which nothing can relieve the individual; and it is a question of absolute dependence upon or rejection of faith's object. The ethicist who does not misunderstand himself cannot be infinitely interested in the reality of another, for he knows that he knows another in terms of possibility, and that is enough; but the Christian believer cannot be content with less than his own reality for the object of his faith, and therefore in the act of faith he leaps over the confines of what he can know; and at the same time the object of belief is itself beyond belief, the existence of God as a particular human being in history. Hence, faith is 'a paradoxical relationship to the paradoxical'.

III

If we suppose for a moment (*pace* all existing philosophers) that Kierkegaard's polemic has clear felled the lower slopes of the philosophic mountain where modern afforestation begins, what would he expect to accrue in the natural regeneration to follow? The thought which sprang up again with a return to the existing individual would be limited but lived (as he said of Greek thought, but with only a small area of it in mind), the primacy of the ethical would be restored; thought would not rule on Olympus but emerge in response to the exigence of the individual, serving to bring him to the point of choosing to will absolutely, thus positing good and evil and bringing into existence a positive self, which in the concrete absolute choice (informed by thought) would become something definite, and by persistence definitive. Instead of being fertilized by thought, will had been choked and forgotten under the thick growth of knowledge, the encyclopaedic mass of information, the infinitude of facts quarried by industrious investigators from inexhaustible natural resources. The only way to vitalize accumulating knowledge and sift its relative importance was to call attention to the neglected *how* of appropriation and ignore the venerated *what* of approximation, raising the question of its relation to the will, to human interests, not least the primary interest of becoming a human being. How an existing individual appropriated truth was the indication of its value. By stressing the *how* Kierkegaard did not mean to offer an operational definition of truth in the practical sense in which scientific truth is defined by the prescribed public procedures of scientific method, which qualifies the *what* of the scientific proposition by the *how* of the way in which it is arrived at and the way in which it is to be used, thus providing the rules for its interpretation and its proof. 'An objective uncertainty held fast in an appropriation-process of the most passionate inwardness is the truth, the highest truth attainable for an *existing* individual.' Such a truth can only be one that is highly relevant to the most cherished interests. The appropriation-process of subjective inwardness is advanced above the approximation-process of objective investigation because that is the vital order and because the age had inverted it, sacrificing life to culture. This concentration of interest upon thought which is strictly relevant to the prime decisions of an existing individual's personal life is Kierkegaard's protest against the age, and that is his excuse for the scandal of effacing the exactitude of the *what* with his qualitative *how*. His recall to first things, just because it is so serious, because it involves him in the drastic reduction of 'thinking and willing one thing', jettisoning the natural sciences, treating history as poetry, confining knowledge of the real to immediate awareness of the ethical reality of the self in the enactment of total decisions, because it is first and last a call to the will, is liable to be mistaken for a technical philosophical subjectivism or for a personal abandonment to the auto-intoxication of choosing to will absolutely, like a young girl in love with love. There is truth in these interpretations, but they are vastly mistaken in so far as they ignore the validity and the primacy of the protest and the recall. Kierkegaard was not contesting the traditional claim of philosophical reflection to guide and guarantee thought and choice; rather, he was employing it in his own way for that purpose. In his own practice, the absolute choice was rationally motivated, the *what* scrupulously determined.

He began with despair, not merely a personal despair but human despair, whether acknowledged or not. When the spontaneity of animal impulse falters and reflection supervenes, will is put in question: whether one wills to be oneself or does not will it, all the possibilities involve one in uncertainties and are dubious in relation to the ground of one's being, a God posited or not posited. To come into reflective existence as a self-conscious being is to despair, for it is a break with the finite, a withdrawal into uncertainty, and yet one has to proceed and without guidance: one is brought to the point of choosing to will absolutely, yet it is impossible to will absolutely any finite end without a contradiction. And it is impossible with any certainty to infer from nature the God of nature. Therefore to hold fast to this objective uncertainty and yet to posit his existence in belief is the only way to choose the infinite with an absolute choice, and to affirm the infinite in oneself. This is the first act of inwardness, the beginning of truth as appropriation. It is made good concretely in an absolute acceptance of the finite self and an absolute renunciation of the finite world, which is nevertheless quietly resumed without perceptible difference in the daily round. The infinite God thus posited in belief in spite of objective uncertainty is at least conceptually possible, but the God-man of history which Christianity claims as the truth is conceptually absurd: the breach with immediacy made by the first act of inwardness is widened immeasurably; the passion of tension created by the uncertainty of the first venture is infinitely increased by this second venture based upon the unintelligible. The intelligible God of reason and the immanent infinity of the individual are abandoned for the God of an historical Incarnation and the conviction of sin. These absolute ventures are total personal decisions taken in absolute loneliness with the utmost responsibility. The authority of another and the example of another are utterly irrelevant; the objective facts, however certain, merely lead one's steps to the edge. To leap or not to leap is inescapably one's own peril. The absolute ethical isolation of the individual in such a decision is for ever irremediable: that is what it meant to be a human being, an existing individual; that is what speculative philosophy, the modern preoccupation with research, the influence of the press, the establishment of Christianity, had obscured and overlaid: Kierkegaard's mature life was 'calculated to make people aware' of just that. Once the total decision is taken, the tension is not relaxed but increased, for nothing has happened to change the situation: faith and reason remain discontinuous, the absurd does not become probable when one decides to build one's life upon it, and with deepening recognition of the risk with repeated renewal of the decision, the suffering is intensified. There is growth in inwardness, but no development of an experience which could confirm the decision and absorb the strain.

If one follows Kierkegaard over this course with any sympathy at all, one must admit that he is ruthlessly rational in discerning and posing the alternatives and following through the consequences to the bitter end. He is guided to his decisions by thought for which he would claim universal validity, although the decisions themselves go beyond thought and are made with the life of a person. Nevertheless, this is a case in which it is easy to trace the line of thought to the peculiarities of the man and his condition. He is socially heterogeneous and jammed in his own introversion; he feels he shares his father's guilt aggravated by his own; he is melancholy and has no sustained appetite for the finite world. A confessed self-torturer, he sadistically inflicts on himself the cruelty of his thought in order to whip up an excitement of will and overcome his *taedium vitae*. There is warrant for such a view in the many passages in which the believer hugs the uncertainty to him so that it wounds him, and would increase it so that it hurt him more, passages in which he perversely makes the truth of inwardness a function of uncertainty, with concomitant variations. All this which made the tragedy of the man does not ruin the validity of his thought, although it is distorted by such excesses. Even if his own will were deficient and supplicated his thought for punishment, he was a demoniac witness to the irreplaceable importance of the reflective will to choose the self absolutely and thus originate a life worthy to be called human, authentic. In the will to will absolutely, that is, without reserve and with all one's life, the individual gives himself a formal determination in which the empirical self is transcended and becomes purified and intensified, a value and a source of value. This formula is more than an adverbial qualification of the Kantian ethical formula which determines the will to will only what can be willed universally, for it integrates both the *how* and the *what*, and it is grounded not merely in abstract reason (which, it was Hegel's criticism of Kant, could never fully rejoin the concrete world) but in the whole personal nature and life of the existing individual. A man can only will absolutely in an original choice, which is also a choice of himself, and which becomes the ground of his subsequent moral decisions.[1]

[1] Kierkegaard's subjectivism is bound to be misunderstood unless one bears in mind that he is really interested in only one thing, viz., a supreme ethical choice. What one shall choose supremely is what one finds it in one to choose supremely, and can be nothing else (although this is not arbitrary and without the guidance of thought). The object of a supreme choice is in the nature of things ideal, uncertainly real; and the more uncertain its reality is the more passionately must

What would have been Kierkegaard's opinion of the determination of this total ethical will offered by Hegel? It is odd that he did not explicitly deal with it, for his polemic against Hegel is a reiterated complaint that Hegel has forgotten he is an existing individual and has left out the ethical. Whereas, of course, Hegel set out to restore the unity of thought and action, the concrete life of the spirit, broken by history, and his philosophic vision of this restoration in history is an appeal to the existing individual to make himself authentic by conscious participation in the historical absolute.

'The very essence of spirit is activity: it realizes its potentiality—makes itself its own deed, its own work—and thus it becomes an object to itself. Thus it is with the spirit of a people, which erects itself into an objective world—a complex of institutions. . . . The relation of the individual to that spirit is that he appropriates to himself this substantial existence; that it becomes his character and capability, enabling him to have a definite place in the world—to be something. For he finds the being of the people to which he belongs an already established, firm world—objectively present to him—with which he has to incorporate himself.' (*Philosophie der Weltgeschichte*).

On Kierkegaard's principle, it might be said that each of them following his own thought had reached a conclusion which, though uncertain, he was prepared to clinch with his life and to live by to the end. But it is not inconsistent with the requirement of decisiveness to attempt to reason out the differences which lead to opposed judgements. Both claim to be guided to their decisions by universally

---

the man hold on to it in subjective inwardness, not in a blind affirmation but, on the contrary, with unrelieved recognition of its objective uncertainty—in the case of the Incarnation, of its intellectual absurdity. Kierkegaard's incisiveness and despair exhibit to full view the scandalous peril of his position. Millions occupy the same position in comfort by leaving the recognition of objective uncertainty on taking a resolution of belief. Such common subjectivism Kierkegaard regarded as the extinction of belief. To depend for one's life upon the object of a supreme choice and to lay hold of it with one hand and with the other to hold on to its objective uncertainty and to hang suspended between the two, that is the meaning of faith; hanging upon them seems to pull them closer together, but that is an illusion which comes of beginning to loose one's hold; grasping them with a firmer grip jerks them violently apart and starts the fierce pain of being torn asunder and the sharp temptation to relinquish one and swing free: that is the subjective inwardness of faith.

valid thought. Kierkegaard certainly rejected Hegel's thought as invalid, because it assumed a standpoint that was inaccessible to an existing individual. Only from a point outside existence would it be possible to survey the totality of existence. Within the process of becoming, the existing individual need not deny the whole, but cannot possibly know the end and survey the whole; his thought suffices only to light up the next step. This judgement applies to the interpretation of world history:

'. . . only by understanding this for oneself can one be led to reconstruct the life of one who is dead, if it really must be done, and if there is time for it. But it is certainly a topsy-turvy notion, instead of learning by living how to recall the life of the dead, to go and try to learn from the dead, apprehended as if they had never lived, how one should (aye, it is inconceivable how topsy-turvy it is) live—as if one were already dead.' (*Concluding Unscientific Postscript*, p. 141.)

His point is that if one goes to history for one's life without having first a life of one's own, one has nothing to go by, no means of discrimination between the authentic and the inauthentic; it is to abdicate the responsibility of living and resort to helpless imitation; it is to be a member of an association, to identify oneself with the age, the nineteenth century, humanity, the public: it is to become a phantom. He would add that if one did first get a life of one's own one would not greatly interest oneself in world history. For he did not believe in history as an objective process revealing God.

'The existing individual who chooses to pursue the objective way enters upon the entire approximation-process by which it is proposed to bring God to light objectively. But this is in all eternity impossible because God is a subject, and therefore exists only for subjectivity in inwardness.' (Ibid., p. 178.)
'As for God, he is never a third party when he is present in the religious consciousness; this is precisely the secret of the religious consciousness.' (Ibid., p. 61.)

Kierkegaard implicitly rejected Hegel's ethic because it was based on false assumptions and because it required an absolute (uncritical) choice of the dead past, but not because it called for humble participation in collective tasks. A particular human being should not wish to dominate others nor to have any special distinction, nor should he seek the illusion of greatness by identifying himself with some collective: 'to will to live as a particular human being . . . in the same sense as is open to every other human being, is the ethical victory over life and all its illusions'. His individualism is not the vulgar refusal to be one amongst many, a drumming on the differential traits. On the contrary, he lays the whole emphasis upon the generically human.

'Every human being must be assumed in essential possession of what essentially belongs to being a man. The task of the subjective thinker is to transform himself into an instrument that clearly and definitely expresses in existence whatever is essentially human.' (Ibid., p. 318.)

His individualism is wholly religious and philosophic, a concentration on the individual as the sole source of the universally human, in reflective willing, authentic choice. He notes the levelling tendency of the age without political feeling; he sees it as playing his own game, forcing the issue, in its tendency either to throw the individual back upon himself, so that he comes to accept himself as one amongst many and learns to be content with himself and to know his individual religious isolation, or else to draw the individual away from himself altogether until he is 'lost in the dizziness of unending abstraction'. He lacked the historical interest and understanding for an adequate analysis of the social situation, but he was saved from a merely literary treatment of it and from personal petulance by his firm anchorage in the religious and philosophic conception of the human situation and the permanent function of the individual in saving and realizing the distinctively human. It is from this point of view that later existentialist thinkers have elaborated their analysis of the modern problem of depersonalization in a mass industrial society. This individualism is as far as possible from a narcissistic attachment to one's ego, a shrinking from the idea of losing oneself in self-transcendence. It was precisely because association with others in a collective venture was not an absolute venture but a substitute for one, 'a fictitious movement of the spirit, a gesture in the direction of the absolute', that Kierkegaard distrusted it.

'In general it is quite inconceivable how ingenious and inventive human beings can be in evading an ultimate decision. Anyone who has seen the curious antics of recruits when they are ordered into the water will often have occasion to perceive analogies in the realm of the spirit.'

The self in so far as it has achieved authentic selfhood in an absolute choice has given itself away absolutely. Extremes meet in Kierkegaard's own peculiar case: his absolute subjectivity becomes absolute objectivity in his total self-displacement before God, which is the effect of his persistence in a reiterated absolute choice of the infinite.

Kierkegaard's case is peculiar. His perpetuation of the moment of absolute choice is morbid, not a perpetuation in a sequence of phases in which the choice is made good in the development of a personality and of a 'work', but a concentration of the whole life in a repetition of the empty abstract decision itself with increasing intensity. This fatal hypertrophy of will has a terrible fascination, for one sees in the dilated organ a living decision repeating itself like an accelerating pulse, separated from the withered body it should have animated. The secret of the case belongs to Kierkegaard's personal tragedy and does not concern the history of thought. For what he bequeathed to philosophy was his protest against 'pure' thought and irrelevant knowledge and his recall to the permanent basis of human living in the ethical isolation of the existing individual.

The will to will absolutely and the idea to think absolutely are indefeasible, but perhaps illegitimate: that is the situation out of which philosophy emerges and with which it has to deal. Kierkegaard, with Hegel's example before him, is cautious about the aspiration to think absolutely. His own example is a caution against the pitfalls which beset the point of absolute choice; but first of all it is (and remains) a summons to make an absolute choice. Because he painfully elaborated in flesh and blood his formidable epigram over Christians and human beings, 'calculated to make people aware', he is the boldest and the greatest of existentialist thinkers.

II

FRIEDRICH NIETZSCHE

(1844–1900)

I

Nietzsche and Kierkegaard are as divided as the poles and as close as twins. Nietzsche cast his supreme choice upon the finite world which Kierkegaard rejected and resigned. Kierkegaard wrote in flesh and blood his epigram, Nietzsche his rhapsody. For both, their drama moved to its inevitable catastrophe: Kierkegaard precipitated himself into the irrevocable either-or of his final unforgivable attack on the Church, Nietzsche into his dionysian nihilism, his euphoria and eventual madness. Both are impossible, mutilated, pitiable; both are formidable and command respect. Both opposed themselves to the culture of the day and returned to the Greeks. Kierkegaard cast himself for the role of Socrates for the salvation of the age; Nietzsche denounced the role of Socrates as the ruin of the age. Both are solitaries, self-driven into desolating isolation. Both are existentialists. For existentialism is not concerned with points of school doctrine but with the recall of philosophy to the existing individual striving to live in the light of reflection, as these pre-eminently did. Nietzsche the existentialist is not the teacher of the Will to Power, Superman, Eternal Recurrence; it is Nietzsche the artist-philosopher and psychologist and critic of culture, above all, Nietzsche the thinker grappling with his own fate. ('It makes the most material difference whether a thinker stands personally related to his problems, having his fate, his need, and even his highest happiness

23

therein; or merely impersonally, that is to say, if he can only feel and grasp them with the tentacles of cold, prying thought.')

The roots of Nietzsche's thinking remain in the Protestant Christianity in which he was bred ('I am the descendant of whole genealogies of Christian clergymen'), in the philosophy of Schopenhauer whom in adolescence he chose for his master, and in the Greek studies in which he was engaged by choice and by profession. However the tree is riven, blasted, and bent, it feeds from these soils and is anchored there. His declaration that God is dead, his reversal of Schopenhauer's ethical judgement, his denunciation of Greek rationalism, these rejections did not separate him from the influences which made him. Thus he posed and lived a problem he could not himself solve. The problem was to overcome scepticism, pessimism, and nihilism; after the undermining of all certainty in respect of knowledge, the lapse of all impulse and goal in respect of will, the extinction of all emotion, to recover intellectual assurance, emotional response, and commanding aims, that was for him the problem of philosophy—joyful wisdom. 'Always, I have written my works with my whole body and life, I do not know what is meant by intellectual problems.' The general disease of nihilism, the *mal de siècle*, the maiming of reason by itself and of will by the Christian ethic, was aggravated in him by the insecure organic basis on which his life rested: hence the desperate push for the sun and the ecstatic vital equilibrium of the dance. 'Out of my will to be in good health, out of my will to live, I have made my philosophy. . . . Self-preservation forbade me to practise a philosophy of wretchedness and discouragement.'

Thus his approach to philosophy and to philosophers is psychological, however technical the problem, for example the problem of knowledge. He asks, what need of the human animal is served by the effort to know and to formulate knowledge? He answers, the need to impose Being (the image of the stable ego) on the process of Becoming. And since the ego, the knowing subject, is also a process, the effort is a falsification, not truth but will, not knowledge but power, for there is strictly no recurrence and therefore strictly no general knowledge, only unique individual relations, perpetual perspectives, interpretations, evaluations. Thus there is no 'thing-in-itself', and nothing has a nature or essence; there is only existence and history. The nearest one gets to the psychological ideal one is striving after in the pursuit of knowledge and devotion to truth is in the persistence of a consistent will cleaving to the same evaluations. This fidelity of the will approximates to stability of Being in the knowing self, and the continued vitality of values approximates to stability of Being in the known world. When a subject can successfully 'create' itself and its object in this way, there is the closest approximation to knowledge; but it is intelligent and necessary falsification, not 'truth': truth is unattainable, and in principle useless. For useful knowledge is a construction, a simplification of the amorphous chaos of impressions and unique relations which is the irreducibly individual truth. Therefore when the principles of knowledge, the rules of this construction, are idealized and made the criterion of 'reality' there follows the radical misunderstanding and falsification characteristic of classical philosophy: 'the world became false precisely owing to the qualities which *constitute its reality*, namely, change, evolution, multifariousness, contrast, contradiction, war'; these were rejected as appearance. Logical ideals (the unity of a systematic whole, consistency, uniformity, etc.) treated as true instead of recognized as useful mean precisely a refusal to accept truth, the real world. The attempt to cancel or transcend the point of view (human or individual) is not to pass from appearance to reality but to postulate a world without relations, unknowable and nonexistent.

This rejection of a transcendent view without perspective, and recall to the selfcreated by its choice and projects and consolidated by commitment and fidelity, as the starting-point of personal reality and the condition of all knowledge, evaluation, and good, is the fundamental position of existentialism. Nietzsche joins Kierkegaard in rejecting the objective Idealism of Hegel, and their acceptance of Kant's subjective Idealism is modified by an irruption of the non-rational displacing his agnosticism. Thought cannot think existence, they agree, but, as Kierkegaard put it, existence 'does not come within the province of thought to think'; above all, thought is not superior to nor a substitute for existence. (Nietzsche goes so far as to speak of consciousness itself as a vulgarization of existence—because its function is to reduce the individual reality to averageness, and he associates the dominance of averaging public thought, as in science, with the dominance of the averaging public, with democracy.) The existing individual thinker realizing his possibilities is the real, and the current of reality flows through him in virtue of his individuality: he joins the real beyond himself not in an act of thought but in thoughtful acts. Thought is secondary, instrumental, subordinate, as Schopenhauer had said.

In spite of his opposing historical existence to essence ('it is only that which has no history which can be defined') and his rejection of the 'thing-in-itself', Nietzsche retained (with his own improvement) Schopenhauer's metaphysical interpretation of the 'thing-in-itself' as impersonal will, the blind striving and strife of things: this was the absolute reality manifested in appearances as thought is embodied in words. In such a world, a world of suffering relieved only by illusion, Schopenhauer's supreme choice was the will not to will. 'A Nihilist is the man who says of the world as it is, that it ought *not* to exist, and of the world as it ought to be, that it does not exist.' Nietzsche wanted to be able to say Yes to this world to which Schopenhauer 'under the dominion of Christian values' had said No. This led him into his immense preoccupation with the critique of morals and of values.

II

The supreme choice which posits good and evil and realizes the ethical reality of the individual is something which Nietzsche sees in the first place historically, in the formation of a particular ethos and culture. A man who can make promises (to himself or another), bind himself for the future, is a late product.

'How thoroughly, in order to be able to regulate the future in this way, must man have first learned to distinguish between necessitated and accidental phenomena, to think causally, to see the distant as present and to anticipate it, to fix with certainty what is the end, and what is the means to that end; above all to reckon, to have power to calculate—how thoroughly must man have first become *calculable*, *disciplined*, *necessitated* even for himself and his own conception of himself, that, like a man entering into a promise, he could guarantee himself *as a future*.' (*The Genealogy of Morals.* Second Essay §1.)

'The sovereign individual, that resembles only himself, . . . the man of the personal, long and independent will, *competent to promise*' is the late fruit of a colossal process in which cruel sanctions were imposed on those who deviated from ' customary morality'. The proud knowledge of responsibility, the consciousness of freedom, power over himself and over fate, Nietzsche calls conscience. The 'bad conscience', the sense of 'guilt', he derives from a different source. The sanctions against the person who failed in what he 'owed', at first the cruel personal revenge of the wronged party, later the impersonal punishment of 'authority', do not induce the 'bad conscience', because the offender accepts his punishment as a fate and does not accuse himself; he is unlucky. It is not until a people is subjugated by a more powerful race that conditions for the 'bad conscience' are provided. Then the natural aggressiveness of the subjugated people is forcibly checked; repressed, it turns inward against the natural life of the human animal. This inhibiting function of thwarted aggression re-deploys the energy of life into other channels and occasions the development of new ideals. (Here Nietzsche anticipates descriptions of the mechanism of conscience, sublimation, and rationalization in the literature of psycho-analysis.)

'This secret self-tyranny, this cruelty of the artist, this delight in giving a form to oneself as a piece of difficult, refractory, and suffering material, in burning in a will, a critique, a contradiction, a contempt, a negation; this sinister and ghastly labour of love on the part of a soul, whose will is cloven in two within itself, which makes itself suffer from delight in the infliction of suffering; this wholly *active* bad conscience has finally (as one already anticipates)—true fountainhead as it is of idealism and imagination—produced an abundance of novel and amazing beauty and affirmation, and perhaps has been the first to give birth to beauty at all.' (Ibid., Second Essay, §18.)

In this way, the altruistic ideals of sympathy, pity, love are born and cultivated amongst a subjugated people, opposed to the egoistic hardy military ideals and virtues of their conquerors, the aristocratic and free persons who impose their will with a good conscience. The ascetic ideal is formed, with its own affirmations and denials.

It is the function of the priest, the ascetic type *par excellence*, himself satisfying his own will to power by his ascendancy and the practice of his arts, scorning rather than hating the men of military power, to divert the resentment of the subjugated by concentrating it upon themselves as the authors of their own miseries, so that they become preoccupied with a God that demands too much, and seek salvation and the consolation of another world, finding in this interpretation of their lot the truth about the human situation in the world, and in obedience and submission the highest good for man. In Nietzsche's view this is the natural protection of the ruling class from contamination by the nausea, the life-negation, and the ideals of the subjugated: it helps them to rule but it also enables them to keep unchallenged their own ideals and virtues. But the cleavage and the protection it affords lasts only for a time, and the characteristic of the modern age is that the ideals and virtues of the subjugated, the priestly ascetic valuations, have prevailed over all: manifest in Schopenhauer's pessimism, in European nihilism, in the dissolution of great traditions, in socialism and the equalitarian ideals of the French Revolution, in democracy and Rousseau's sentimental idealization of the natural man. Most serious of all, it is manifest in the proudest achievement of the modern age, in science. At the end of *The Genealogy of Morals*, Nietzsche asks, ' Where is the *counterpart* of this complete system of will, end, and interpretation? Where is the other " one aim"? ' The generally accepted answer is that the cool self-sufficiency and persistent success of modern science point the alternative aim and system of values. It is not Nietzsche's answer.

'When science is not the latest manifestation of the ascetic ideal—but these are cases of such rarity, selectness, and exquisiteness, as to preclude the general judgement being affected thereby—science is a *hiding-place* for every kind of cowardice, disbelief, remorse, *despectio sui*, bad conscience—it is the very *anxiety* that springs from having no ideal, the suffering from the *lack* of a great love, the discontent with an enforced moderation. Oh, what does all science not cover to-day? How much, at any rate, does it not try to cover? The diligence of our best scholars, their senseless industry, their burning the candle of their brain at both ends—their very mastery of their handiwork—how often is the real meaning of all that to prevent themselves continuing to see a certain thing? Science as self-anaesthetic: do you know that?' (Ibid., Third Essay, §23.)

Modern science, like Hegel's world-history and Schopenhauer's compassion, was one of the many elaborate ways in which the modern individual took refuge from himself and sought to lose himself and dodge the decisive struggles of human destiny. The exacting discipline of a strict agnosticism, the renunciation of all interpretation, may amount to an heroic devotion, even then it is faith in the ascetic ideal, for it is faith in a metaphysical value, an intrinsic value of truth—to which the self is to be sacrified. '. . . in every department science needs an ideal value, a power which creates values, and in whose *service* it *can believe* in itself—science itself never creates values'. Thus science for its own sake is the latest development of the ascetic ideal which renounces life tortuously.

'Everywhere . . . where the mind is at work seriously, powerfully, and without counterfeiting, it dispenses altogether now with an ideal (the popular expression for this abstinence is "Atheism")—*with the exception of the will for truth*. But this will, this *remnant* of an ideal, is, if you will believe me, that ideal itself in its severest and cleverest formulation, esoteric through and through, stripped of all outworks, and consequently not so much its remnant as its *kernel* . . . .

'After Christian truthfulness has drawn one conclusion after the other, it finally draws its strongest conclusion, its conclusion against itself; this, however, happens when it puts the question, *what is the meaning of every will for truth?* . . . what sense has our whole being, if it does not mean that in our own selves that will for truth has come to its own consciousness *as a problem*? . . . . By reason of this attainment of self-consciousness on the part of the will for truth, morality from henceforward—there is no doubt about it—goes *to pieces*; this is that great hundred-act play that is reserved for the next two centuries of Europe, the most terrible, the most mysterious, and perhaps also the most hopeful of all plays.' (Ibid., Third Essay, §27.)

The ascetic ideal forced to its last refuge in the will to truth is compelled to accept the need for interpretations and valuations which it had renounced, and this means alternatives to established moralities: Nothing is true, everything is allowed', that esoteric principle of the elect. Or else it must choose suicidal nihilism. But such an open-eyed choice is the most difficult of all.

'It is absolutely impossible to disguise *what* in point of fact is made clear by every complete will that has taken its direction from the ascetic ideal; this hate of the human, and even more of the animal, and more still of the material, this horror of the senses, of reason itself, this fear of happiness and beauty, this desire to get right away from all illusion, change, growth, death, wishing and even desiring— all this means—let us have the courage to grasp it—a will for Nothingness, a will opposed to life, a repudiation of the most fundamental conditions of life, but it is and remains *a will*! and to say at the end that which I said at the beginning—man will wish Nothingness rather than not wish *at all*.' (Ibid., Third Essay, §28.)

The disgust for life, the nausea, the turning away, which arises primarily amongst a subjugated people whose aggressiveness is turned inwards, but which has also plenty of other causes and conditions, becomes itself a theme, an interpretation giving a meaning to life and suffering, an organized purpose, a form of will and being. It produces much that is beautiful and best, but when it becomes the major theme, the dominant and exclusive interpretation, a blight on the positive instincts and primal energies, then life is sick, goodness is called evil and evil good.

It is certainly not Nietzsche's purpose merely to celebrate and to restore the aristocratic or Greek virtues and values and to denigrate Christian virtues and values, however encouraged by his panegyrics would-be strong men may have been; it is not his purpose merely to glorify the good conscience of the pagan or machiavellian and to deplore the bad conscience of the Christian: this he does as part of his purpose in effecting a critique of all values and virtues, showing the source of all alike, openly or secretly, in will, the will to power. His purpose as a philosopher is to counter the bias, the establishments, the illusions of the age, to raise the questions and set the problems. Morality becomes a problem because neither the machiavellian or pagan good conscience nor the Christian bad conscience is any longer possible: the Christian faith has been undermined and has collapsed, and with it the entire European morality. The first thing to be done is to recognize what this means, to draw the uttermost deductions: 'every hazard is again permitted to the discerner; the sea, *our* sea, again lies open before us; perhaps never before did such an "open sea" exist'.

Kierkegaard had not believed that it was possible to discern directly a divine order either in nature or in history, but what he most objected to in Hegel was the attempt to rationalize the Christian religion, to assign it to its place in a grandiose rationale of history. Nietzsche's objection is the same as Schopenhauer's, the objection of the atheist: 'the non-divinity of existence was regarded by him [Schopenhauer] as something understood, palpable, indisputable'. On such premises, the question is: '*Has existence then a significance at all?* . . . the question which will require a couple of centuries even to be completely heard in all its profundity'. Schopenhauer's own answer, his moral condemnation of life, was premature because it derived from the Christian moral values, themselves the product of a long history in which Christian belief had played a leading part. Nietzsche, having examined the origin of those values, and wanting to say Yes to life, is able to begin to rejoice in evil, as designated by the ascetic ideal, to look beyond good and evil. Consciousness, in any case, is not the last word, the final authority; its generalized and vulgarized world is not superior to the unconscious world within oneself and in nature, in matter. Respect for and trust in the dynamics of the unconscious world, reduction of the value of the conscious and knowable: these are the dangerous but necessary thoughts which threaten the throne and challenge the rule of classical philosophy. Moreover, Nietzsche's rejection of Christian belief and criticism of Christian moral values is not at all made from the standpoint of a scientific materialist, who merely assumes 'belief in a world which is supposed to have its equivalent and measure in human thinking and human valuations, a "world of truth" at which we might be able ultimately to arrive with the help of our insignificant, four-cornered human reason!' Valuation and interpretation are questions far too open to be foreclosed by scientific results. Nor can there be any complacent assumptions; the answers are rooted in will, and what is one man's highest hope may well be to another a distasteful possibility (as Herbert Spencer's vision of progress was to Nietzsche).

III

Nietzsche discerns the problem of values as presented for the first time, and therefore as a crisis in the destiny of man, the most important in all history. Hitherto, values have been historically determined; now man has become reflective and must take upon himself the full burden of responsibility and freedom.

'As soon as . . . no thinker can any longer relieve his conscience with the hypothesis "God or eternal values", the claim of the law-giver to determine new values rises to an awfulness which has not yet been experienced.' (*The Will to Power*, 972.)

'O my brethren, when I enjoined on you to break up the good, and the tables of the good, then only did I embark man on his high seas.

'And now only cometh to him the great terror, the great outlook, the great sickness, the great nausea, the great sea-sickness.' (*Thus Spake Zarathustra*, LVI. 28.)

'. . . one could imagine a delight and a power of self-determining, and a *freedom* of will whereby a spirit could bid farewell to every belief, to every wish for certainty, accustomed as it would be to support itself on slender cords and possibilities, and to dance even on the verge of abysses.' (*The Joyful Wisdom*, 347.)

Nevertheless, this dizzy position in which modern man finds himself when he is awakened by reflective criticism is not merely a personal predicament. Values are a slow-maturing product of ages of social discipline.

'. . . everything of the nature of freedom, elegance, boldness, dance, and masterly certainty, which exists or has existed, whether it be in thought itself, or in administration, or in speaking and persuading, in art just as in conduct, has only developed by means of the tyranny of such arbitrary law; and in all seriousness, it is not at all improbable that precisely this is "nature and natural"—and *not laisser-aller . . .* !

' "Thou must obey someone, and for a long time; *otherwise* thou wilt come to grief, and lose all respect for thyself"—this seems to me to be the moral imperative of nature . . . to nations, races, ages, and ranks, above all, however, to the animal "man" generally, to *mankind.*' (*Beyond Good and Evil*, 188.)

Selected virtues and graces in the maturity of a social tradition flower in spontaneous free persons, who because of their happy constitution, the fruit of this long discipline, are begetters and bestowers of value, the emanation of their radiant virtue. Such results are the outcome of ages of breeding, training, and tradition, beyond the conscious power of the individual. The reflective person, the philosopher, cannot by taking thought win for himself or others this unreflective power which is the happy gift of history—any more than the brain can replace the somatic mechanisms and processes on which it depends. What the philosopher can do is to understand the conditions of health and diagnose the disease of the age, and attempt to bring into existence conscious movements which will counteract any fatal tendency of the times. Reflective analysis brings to light the underlying conditions which have produced greatness in the past and reveals conditions which threaten greatness in the present and in the future. The role of the philosopher is to warn and bear witness and exemplify, but not to invent values or produce them out of his consciousness.

'. . . it seems to us at present absolutely ridiculous when a man claims to devise values *to surpass* the values of the actual world.' (*The Joyful Wisdom*, 346.)

'According to what standard is the objective value measured? According to the quantity of *increased* and *more organized* power alone.' (*The Will to Power*, 674.)

'The concept, "the other world", suggests that this world *might be different*—it suppresses necessity and fate (it is useless to *submit* and to *adapt oneself*).' (*The Will to Power*, 586.)

'The kind of *experimental philosophy* which I am living, even anticipates the possibility of the most fundamental Nihilism, on principle: but by this I do not mean that it remains standing at a negation, at a *no*, or at a will to negation. It would rather attain to the very reverse—to a *Dionysian affirmation* of the world, as it is, without subtraction, exception, or choice—it would have eternal circular motion: the same things, the same reasoning, and the same illogical concatenation. The highest state to which a philosopher can attain: to maintain a Dionysian attitude to Life—my formula for this is *amor fati*.' (*The Will to Power*, 1041.)

Nietzsche takes the will to power (it is Schopenhauer's metaphysical will as the absolute nature of all existence—given content and direction) as the necessary and abiding source of all possible values, even the life-denying ones. The great difference between cultures and value-systems is between those which say Yes and those which say No to life, understood as will in this sense. Those which say No unavoidably manifest the same will, and produce virtues and values which glorify man, but the persistence of such cultures until their ideal universally prevails systematically checks the will to power by dividing it against itself, and therefore enfeebles man and threatens chronic degeneration. Europe under such a system has produced objectivity, the scientific spirit, and the ideal of love, but threatens to reduce all mankind to a level of green-meadow gregariousness, contentment, ease, security, and bovine mediocrity. Science and democracy are not the modern awakening from the illusions of Christian faith and order, they are the same ascetic valuations in their most viable modern form; they lead to gregarious inertia, mass similarity, equality, and nonentity (mankind turned into sand, 'small, soft, round, infinite sand'), the extinction of all interest, splendour, and quality in human life; finally, ennui and extinction of the will to live. This is a notion in the moral world comparable to the notion in the physical world of thermo-dynamic equilibrium, the running down of the universe to an irreversible heat-death. Is the moral process equally irreversible? Kierkegaard had the same vision of the tendency of the age, which reached its limit in an 'unlimited panorama of abstract infinity, unrelieved by even the smallest eminence, undisturbed by even the slightest interest, a sea of desert'. Concerned only with the individual and his choice of eternity and believing that such conditions would help to drive the individual back on himself and thus renew the true differential, the only source of vitality, he was not disturbed. But Nietzsche, fixing his choice on the finite and remembering the past, is roused: ' he who divines the fate that is hidden under the idiotic unwariness and blind confidence of "modern ideas", and still more under the whole of Christo-European morality —suffers from an anguish with which no other is to be compared'. The levelling process should even be accelerated, but with it should go the counter-measures; first, to restore respect for the virtues and values of the direct expression of the will to power of those who know life for what it is and say Yes to it; then the long preparation of an *élite* with privileged interests and endowed advantage, separated from the herd by the pathos of distance.

'Not only a ruling race whose task would be consummated in ruling alone: but a race with *vital spheres* of its own, with an overflow of energy for beauty, bravery, culture, and manners, even for the most abstract thought; a yea-saying race which would be able to allow itself every kind of great luxury—strong enough to be able to dispense with the tyranny of the imperatives of virtue, rich enough to be in no need of economy or pedantry; beyond good and evil; a forcing-house for rare and exceptional plants.' (*The Will to Power*, 898.)

'One must appeal to immense opposing forces in order to thwart this natural, all-too-natural *progressus in simile*, the evolution of man to the similar, the ordinary, the average, the gregarious—to the ignoble!' (*Beyond Good and Evil*, 268.)

There can be no deliberate going back, but the fundamental duality persists: the superabundant vitality and the reduced vitality, the conquerors and the conquered, the herd man and the solitary choice spirit, the Dionysian ideal of vitality and the Apollonian ideal of form, the Greek and the Christian. The antagonism of Dionysus and Apollo can be resolved, and was resolved by the Greeks in their greatest triumphs, but the antagonism of the Dionysian ideal and the Christian admits of no compromise; it is an Either-Or, the Yes or No to life. In our time it is not enough to drop Christianity and go on as before, for everything that remains is Christian; it is necessary 'to *overcome* everything Christian by something super-Christian, and not only to rid oneself of it—for Christian doctrine is the counter-doctrine of the Dionysian'. This super-Christian doctrine is the doctrine of Superman: man is to be surpassed. This is the supreme choice, the commanding aim.

The other myth of Nietzsche's, revealed to him in a moment of illumination, his doctrine of Eternal Recurrence, expresses the crass senselessness of things, the eternal lack of *telos* in the universe; so that to will the eternal cycle with enthusiasm and without hope is the ultimate attainment of affirmation—*amor fati*. Compare Kierkegaard's eulogy of Repetition.

'Whoever fails to understand that life is repetition, and that this is its beauty, has passed judgement upon himself; he deserves no better fate than that which will befall him, namely to be lost. Hope is an alluring fruit which does not satisfy, memory is a miserable pittance that does not satisfy, but repetition is life's daily bread, which satisfies and blesses. When a man has circumnavigated the globe it will appear whether he has the courage to understand that life is repetition, and the enthusiasm to find therein his happiness. . . . In repetition inheres the earnestness and reality of life. Whoever wills repetition proves himself to be in possession of a pathos that is serious and mature.' (*Repetition*.)

Repetition is an essential and recurrent ideal in existentialist thinking. Marcel's fidelity, Heidegger's interest in the reaffirmation of primitive philosophical questions, the rhythm of withdrawal and choice in Jaspers or Sartre, are merely the most obvious examples of this characteristic of a philosophy which is interested only in exploring and deepening individually realized experiences. Whether in Lucretius or in a modern, this idea is not likely to be far from the centre of a personal philosophy which is more reflective than romantic. At first sight, Nietzsche's Eternal Recurrence is the opposite of all this, a destructive delight in the acceptance of absurdity, not a poetic destruction of the familiar; but for Nietzsche Eternal Recurrence was an illumination, a release, a discovery, perhaps not far different spiritually from the illumination of later existentialists on the road of negation.

IV

The aphoristic and the dithyrambic forms of most of Nietzsche's writings represent very well the darting and intuitive and the mocking, singing, and dancing manner and method of his mind. There is no lack of nuance and of subtlety, nor of ambition.

'To have travelled throughout the entire extent of the modern soul, to have taken my meals in each of its corners, my pride, my torment, my joy.

'To overcome pessimism effectively and, at last, to look with the eyes of a Goethe full of love and goodwill.' (*The Will to Power*, 1031.)

But, like Kierkegaard, he was too explosive a mixture to mature: 'I am one of those materials which can burst'. He was not a Thersites, for he was formed on the virtues and values he made it his mission to denounce. The undergraduate and the master are compounded in him rather than mixed. In the nature of the case, he was not likely to be lucky in his followers ('A teacher must not be judged by his first disciples'). He is the perfect course over which to try out one's maturity: one might say he is necessary to the maturing of a modern spirit.

He is an existentialist in his taking the problems of his philosophy from the conflicts of the age instead of from the disputes of the schools. To make himself profoundly representative of his time and to surmount its problems in himself in public was his aim in philosophy, an aim which produces not systems or doctrines but a sharpening of awareness, a deepening of understanding, an orientation, a quickening of new possibilities.

'Will they be new friends of "truth", these coming philosophers? Very probably, for all philosophers hitherto have loved their truths. But assuredly they will not be dogmatists. It must be contrary to their pride, and also contrary to their taste, that their truth should still be truth for everyone—that which hitherto has been the secret wish and ultimate purpose of all dogmatic efforts. "My opinion is *my* opinion: another person has not easily a right to it"—such a philosopher of the future will say, perhaps.' (*Beyond Good and Evil*, 43.)

This playful spitting in the face of the goddess of intellectual idolatry is one way of rudely calling public attention to the insufficiency of public knowledge, which is the constant theme of existentialists. Marcel opposes the *pensée pensante* to the *pensée pensée*. Kierkegaard hides himself, saying, 'next to knowing whether I have any opinion or not, nothing could very well be of less importance to another than the knowledge of what that opinion might be'. The inwardness of an opinion is part and parcel of its truth, all that belongs to it on the side of the personal search for it and the use to which it is put. The portrait of the objective spirit, the disinterested investigator (in contrast to the philosopher who commits himself and takes his stand and his aim in the light of the relevant alternatives) has never been better done than by Nietzsche, especially (in the manner of La Bruyère) in *Beyond Good and Evil*, 207, and in 'The Land of Culture' (*Zarathustra* II, XXXVI) and 'Immaculate Perception' (*Zarathustra* II, XXXVII). Objectivity is not repudiated but is given an existentialist ground.

'. . . the very seeing of another vista, the very *wishing* to see another vista, is no little training and preparation of the intellect for its eternal "Objectivity"—objectivity being understood not as "contemplation without interest" (for that is inconceivable and nonsensical), but as the ability to have the pros and cons *in one's power* and to switch them on and off, so as to get to know how to utilize, for the advancement of knowledge, the *difference* in the perspective and in the emotional interpretations. But let us, forsooth, my philosophical colleagues, henceforward guard ourselves more carefully against this mythology of dangerous ancient ideas, which has set up a "pure, will-less, painless, timeless subject of knowledge"; let us guard ourselves from the tentacles of such contradictory ideas as "pure reason", "absolute spirituality, knowledge-in-itself ". . . . There is only a seeing from a perspective, only a "knowing" from a perspective, and the *more* emotions we express over a thing, the *more* eyes, different eyes, we train on the same thing, the more complete will be our 'idea' of that thing, our "objectivity". But the elimination of the will altogether, the switching off of the emotions all and sundry, granted that we could do so, what! would not that be called intellectual *castration*?' (*The Genealogy of Morals*. Third Essay, 12.)

Similarly, objectivity in the aesthetic field cannot properly abstract from the individuality of subject and object.

'Kant thought that he showed honour to art when he favoured and placed in the foreground those of the predicates of the beautiful which constitute the honour of knowledge: impersonality and universality. This is not the place to discuss whether this was not a complete mistake; all that I wish to emphasize is that Kant, just like other philosophers, instead of envisaging the aesthetic problem from the standpoint of the experiences of the artist (the creator), has only considered art and beauty from the standpoint of the spectator. . . . But if only the philosophers of the beautiful had sufficient knowledge of this "spectator"! Knowledge of him as a great fact of personality, as a great experience, as a wealth of strong and most individual events, desires, surprises, and raptures in the sphere of beauty!' (*The Genealogy of Morals*. Third Essay, 6.)

These major themes of existentialism are supported by some of the minor themes scattered throughout the works of Nietzsche. For example: the way in which people become identified with their role in life and lose or forget their personal possibilities in playing a part (*Joyful Wisdom*, 356); or the various ways in which, having failed to become ourselves, we become an impersonal third party, or the phantom which flits in the opinions others have of us, and live under the rule of an abstraction we invent called 'man' (*The Joyful Wisdom*, 368; *The Dawn of Day*, 105); or the impossibility of knowing another save as an object which is not he (*The Dawn of Day*, 118). He had no knowledge of Kierkegaard, and his own supreme choice, equally extreme, was the precise contrary, but he had perfect insight into the possibility of Kierkegaard.

'Faith, such as early Christianity desired, and not infrequently achieved in the midst of a sceptical and southernly free-spirited world, which had centuries of struggle between philosophical schools behind it and in it, counting besides the education in tolerance which the *imperium Romanum* gave—this faith is *not* that sincere, austere slave-faith by which perhaps a Luther or a Cromwell, or some other northern barbarian of the spirit remained attached to his God and Christianity; it is much rather the faith of Pascal, which resembles in a terrible manner a continuous suicide of reason—a tough, long-lived, wormlike reason, which is not to be slain at once and with a single blow. The Christian faith from the beginning is sacrifice: the sacrifice of all freedom, all pride, all self-confidence of spirit; it is at the same time subjection, self-derision, and self-mutilation. There is cruelty and religious Phoenicianism in this faith, which is adapted to a tender, many-sided, and very fastidious conscience; it takes for granted that the subjection of the spirit is indescribably *painful*, that all the past and all the habits of such a spirit resist the *absurdissimum*, in the form of which "faith" comes to it. Modern men, with their obtuseness as regards Christian nomenclature, have no longer the sense for the terribly superlative conception which was implied to an antique taste by the paradox of the formula, "God on the Cross".'

(*Beyond Good and Evil*, 46.)

Nietzsche's work is to complete the circle of nineteenth-century European scepticism and pessimism, to round it out to a full nihilism, as the necessary preliminary to anything else. In particular he wishes to destroy the nineteenth-century illusion that Christian faith can be quietly dropped like the belief in fairies, and everything else remain as before. Christian beliefs might flicker and go out but the moral consciousness, fount of our intuitions and secret source of our unshakable convictions and unquestioned assumptions, was saturated with generations of Christian prejudice: of this, Schopenhauer was the great example. And classical philosophy had been no less deceived and deceiving than Christian faith: it had wished to show the cosmic world as a rational system, an entelechy, a teleology, whereas reality was multifarious, inconsistent, absurd; it had been built to buttress the main fabric of morality, in spite of the ingrained opposition to morality of all nature and history. No philosophy could count which persisted in building these abstract illusions as a refuge from the reality of individual experience. To bring this home, it was necessary above all to cut off the retreat of the agnostics to the independent position of ethics, the impregnable bastion of morality.

(Of course mankind had not waited until Nietzsche to discover the conflict of values, the inexpurgatory ambiguity of good and of evil; so profound a fact was as inescapable as fate and as perpetually obscured and hushed up as a family scandal. It had come to light often enough, notably in Thucydides and Macchiavelli and Hobbes on the political side, and in the French moralists of the seventeenth century on the psychological and personal side. Since Nietzsche, it has come to the surface in our own time with a vengeance, in the clinic and on the stage of history. The conflict of moral ideals in politics is sharply expressed by the sensitive conscience of Max Weber thus:

'There are two fundamentally different ethical conceptions: the ethics of sentiment and the ethics of responsibility. . . . The believer in an absolute ethic cannot stand up to the ethical irrationality of the world. He who enters politics concludes a pact with devilish powers, since it is a realm where alone power and violence are valid means; yet from good may come evil and from evil good. Who does not see this is politically a child.')

Plato had found one answer after another to the contention that justice is the prevailing will of the strong not the countervailing conspiracy of the weak to defraud the strong, and was dissatisfied with them all until his attempt at a definitive answer in the *Republic*. Nietzsche re-opened the debate without Plato's anxiety to secure the triumph of the 'right' side; on the contrary, with the intention of really putting the issue in question, and without the means to find any satisfactory answer at all. Yet his attack on established assumptions was from the point of view of the moralist and for the sake of morality; like Kierkegaard, he was interested in the *how*, the assumptions, motives, and point of view of contemporary morality. He wanted a self-authenticated, self-disciplined, heroic morality, with all its risk and responsibility, whatever its content. It was as necessary and as difficult to become moral as to become a Christian in Kierkegaard's sense.

In his own case, he provided himself with no means of getting out of the nihilism into which he plunged himself, precisely because it was a deliberate plunge over the edge. He tried to say at the same time: nihilism must be surmounted; nihilism cannot be surmounted; nihilism is good, nihilism is best. He imprisoned himself within the chalked circle of his own metaphysical assumptions. His excursions into the natural history of morals and his psychological analysis brilliantly anticipated the scientific research in anthropology and psychology which has so vastly influenced the moral outlook in our day, but his insight and his judgement did not avail to save or to serve himself. For his thinking was ancillary to the real philosophic task he set himself of experimentally *living* all the valuations of the past, together with their contraries, in order to acquire the right to judge them. This dangerous existentialist counsel of perfection at least refuses to recognize any criterion of value outside human experience of satisfaction, and this ought to have exorcized the metaphysical will to power which bedevilled Nietzsche's thinking; but he himself refused to accept consistently this criterion implicit in his experimentalism, 'man as the standard of the value of things': man must adapt himself to existence or abolish himself—that was the whole disjunction of life, a choice between two forms of nihilism. There are positions which can be thought but not lived, there are exploratory ventures from which there is no return. Nietzsche's thoughts were fascinated by unexplored forbidden regions of abysses, glaciers, and mountain peaks. One can look down into the bottom of an abyss refusing the possibility of throwing oneself over the edge, but one cannot explore the possibility by a tentative jump. One can examine in thought the possibility of nihilism (as an irresolvable conflict between human valuations and cosmic facts) and try to show that it is not the truth; but if one is determined to will and to live the possibility of nihilism, then one no longer has any independent standpoint under one's feet; worse than Kierkegaard 'out upon the seventy thousand fathoms of water', one is actually sucked down and engulfed: what from the independent standpoint of responsible freedom was recognized as the unavoidable ambiguity of good and of evil in the world becomes, first, the ambiguity of one's own will, and then its abandonment to the eternal destruction and the eternal return and the dionysian ecstasy. No more than scepticism can be overcome by doubting it can nihilism be overcome by willing it.

Nietzsche began the building of his intellectual home with the invention, taste, and boldness of a master, but he became involved in neologism and travesty, and at last it stood unachieved, like a ruin, open to the four winds and to the sun and the rain. Only the most foolish of his followers have attempted to occupy it. More vividly than any, he exemplifies the existentialist truth that a philosopher who tries to make himself representative and seriously builds himself a habitation to suit his own intimately understood needs does not offer a home to others but may enormously enrich the resources out of which others build for their own convenience and dignity.

III

KARL JASPERS

(Born 1883)

I

BOTH Kierkegaard and Nietzsche compared themselves to a lonely fir. They were indeed, and perhaps in spite of themselves, solitaries: boulders which worked loose from the mass of human solidarity, and crashed to the bottom. In Karl Jaspers we see them deflecting the course of traditional philosophy. For Jaspers is the professional philosopher inheriting and participating in the *philosophia perennis* 'around which all philosophers circle', and at the same time he is profoundly influenced by Kierkegaard and Nietzsche. He treats them as the great exceptions. He is not a disciple (they cannot be followed), but he makes it his enterprise to profit by their intuitions and apply them to the business of philosophy, in the spirit of a true philosopher reflecting upon his own effort to live and living in the light of his reflections.

Philosophy, Jaspers feels, cannot be the same after Kierkegaard and Nietzsche because they have awakened us to our human condition, as Hume changed philosophy by awakening us to the state of our knowledge. Theirs is a challenge to our assumptions about ourselves as persons. They have raised the question, what does it mean to be a human being; and what does it mean to be a Christian, or not to be a Christian? But their approach also put in question philosophy itself, for how can descriptions and formulations have universal validity and intelligibility and also remain close to the authenticity and even eccentricity of individual experience? And further, and most important of all, if ultimate reality is not an object of conceptual thought, how can experience of it be made veridical, intelligible, and communicable? How can philosophy supply the norms which individual experience seeks, if it confines itself to the evocative value, the appeal and witness, of individual experience? Can there be philosophy, or only autobiography?

Classical philosophy comes to an end in Hegel, because it has become folly to construct intellectual totalitarian systems in which everything is taken up, harmonized, rationalized, and justified. Such palaces are still marvellous, but nobody can live in them. The savour and reality of human existence, its perils and triumphs, its bitterness and sweetness, are outside in the street.[1]

Nevertheless, the reaction against metaphysics has not yet brought anything better, nearer to the plenitude and reality of experience. Some have resolved philosophy into science, that is to say, made philosophical claims for science or sought a philosophy of life in science. Others have resorted again to religious dogma, to save the life of the emotions and the imagination. This superstitious cult of science or of religion can only be remedied by a return to philosophy. But that will make confusion worse confounded unless philosophers have learned their lesson: they must know how to define the limits of science and at the same time recognize that science is the definition and standard of objective knowledge. Philosophy cannot again pretend to be universal knowledge. We have lost our naïvety; for we recognize the discontinuities in the realm of Being, which the old systems took as one and treated as the object of universal knowledge, answerable to the structure of thought. The modern starting-point, and the strength of our position, is in the recognition of this discontinuity between the three forms of Being: being-there, being-oneself, being-in-itself. These forms of Being are explored by different methods. The philosopher living his life participates in all three. Philosophy must make and keep the separation and develop the methods of exploration appropriate to each.

---

[1] Cp. Simone de Beauvoir, *Pour une morale de l'ambiguité*, p. 221, 'I remember having felt a great calm in reading Hegel in the impersonal setting of the Bibliothèque Nationale, in August 1940. But when I found myself again in the street, in my life, outside the system, under a real sky, the system was no longer any use to me: it was, under the pretext of the infinite, the consolations of death which it had offered me; and I still wanted to live in the midst of living men.'

II

Jaspers starts with the assumption that there is a given external world in which the thinker has foothold, a world of stable objects which compel and control the adherence of knowledge. This world of science is one in which everything known is an object (in the sense that it is experienced as stable and registered in a communicable representation), and is objective (in the sense that what is known about it is universally intelligible and accepted). Science, then, is a relation between an intelligible world and human understanding as such: 'all knowledge and every object in the world is for consciousness in general'.

This objective knowledge of what is there (being-there) is assumed by many to be the whole ambition of human thought, because it is assumed that there is nothing which is not given in stable objects registered in the human mind in representations which in logical order are universally intelligible and communicable. Therefore science is the measure of all things. 'This objective certainty which maintains itself without my concurrence, and before which every form of my subjectivity has no standing and is dissolved, is the very image of all that is solid. In laying hold of it I feel an incomparable satisfaction.' The quest for certainty is supported by the fear of liberty; for the anxieties and risks of personal responsibility and decision are escaped if all can be reduced to a necessary and universal objectivity: liberty and choice imply the imperfection of knowledge—uncertainty. Descartes, on the threshold of modern philosophy, enunciating his *Cogito*, announced himself as an individual thinker looking out upon the world from his necessary solitude, an existentialist, but went on to refuse to take the risks inseparable from his recognized position, and took refuge from himself in dogmas: his pronouncement turned out to be merely a recourse of method, not a personal recognition of the possibility of despair, and the reality of liberty.

In what way does the objective knowledge established by science fall short? Reason is not satisfied with clarity, and aims also at unity and totality of knowledge. Objectivity, fully realized, is knowledge complete and exclusive.

Science is incapable in principle of achieving this ideal of objectivity. If it were realized, the world would be exhaustively intelligible to human consciousness as such. But there are vital forms of consciousness lying, as it were, above and below the level of public knowledge and incapable of being wholly reduced to its forms and norms: the more or less obscure and fugitive sensations, perceptions, feelings, intuitions, intimations of the private consciousness, which are in part the raw material of public knowledge and in part are intractable to scientific method, and responsive to unpredictable manifestations of reality; and the uniquely personal self-determination of the free personality. These vitally important elements pass through the filter of the most resourceful and perfected science.

Further, inductive knowledge can never be more than probable, and in some fields must remain indefinite. It cannot have either a beginning or an end. It is impossible to form out of scientific concepts a coherent image of the world: it has never been successfully maintained that the world is at bottom number, or matter, or spirit, or energy, or any other comprehensive idea borrowed from any of the sciences studying a coherent body of phenomena. Nor can the sciences be systematized into a comprehensive unity, although it must always remain a legitimate, and indeed necessary, scientific enterprise to make the attempt. There is no science which can gain hegemony by subsuming all others under itself. Especially is there an irreducible difference between the sciences of nature and of man. The sciences of man, of which history is a type, are meaningless, a dust of unrelated facts, unless they are more than science, for they require a comprehension of ideas, an appreciation of ethos, a reconstruction in which the mind of the scholar participates; and such an interpretation of the data can never be final: history is always contemporary. Ideas can never in any field of science be finally objective, in the sense of wholly taking the place of the individual facts to which they direct attention or which they summarize or which they elucidate.

The hope of complete objectivity is linked to the hope of utopia, a final victory over man's practical problems. Both are illusory; both imply the hope of reducing all things to mechanics and manufacture. Neither the world nor knowledge is a unity, not to say a unity of that kind. There is no refuge from the hazards of real life in such illusions.

Science, then, achieves the clarity and universality of objective knowledge, but cannot attain the unity and totality to which reason aspires. The sciences are empirical and must work as best they can. It is not for the philosopher to give them rules nor practical limits. The limits which he defines are ultimate principles; what they can achieve in their own fields is always open and indefinite. Science which understands itself and recognizes its ultimate limits is itself

46

philosophy because it is animated by the same spirit, the will to know, the persistent attempt to think clearly, the quest for reality; and because there is no other world than the world which science describes.

Science is therefore the necessary ground and first stage of philosophy, but is not capable of achieving the unity and totality which reason cannot renounce. Science is concerned with determinate being and the philosopher beginning with science comes up against its limits, recognizes that he can neither think absolute being nor renounce the will to think it; he is forced to reflect: 'it is thinkable that there may be an unthinkable'. Philosophy cannot add anything to the objective knowledge of science. Philosophy begins with the philosopher's existence, with what he is, not with what he knows; he achieves and communicates not knowledge but himself. The unity and totality which philosophy recognizes that science can never achieve belong to the world in its transcendence (being-in-itself), to which the thinker has access only by means of his own transcendence (being-oneself) of the empirical world (being-there). The thinker participates in all three realms of being and by that means alone can approach the unity and totality to which his reason aspires, never by trying to reduce everything to the universally intelligible order of being-there. Nothing is more philosophical than science when it abjures metaphysics and is faithful in attention to its own empirical pursuits, for in its docility and persistence it is then near the authentic reality to which it aspires. But to say this is to shift the accent from science to the scientific worker, who is himself the authentic philosopher when he is going about his own business with understanding and purpose. Philosophy begins with science and cannot do without it, because there is no other world independent of the objective world which science explores. 'Only one who has passionately given himself up to the exploration of the world can find access to philosophy.' Philosophy which is dissociated from the world is lost.

From his standpoint of the separation of the three orders of Being, Jaspers is able to disentangle the confusion of philosophy and science which interferes with the effectiveness of each. Beginning with a criticism of this confusion in Descartes, he can show the dogmatism and vanity of positivism in reducing all philosophy to science, the sterility of idealism in reducing all science to philosophy, the fatal neglect of science in Kierkegaard's leap into transcendence, the stultification of philosophy by Nietzsche's importation of biological concepts. So strong is his position that he can treat the two most

KARL JASPERS

characteristic forms of confusion in the relations of science and philosophy, the reduction of one to the other, positivism and idealism,
with generous appreciation of the truths and values for which each
contends. The effect of his criticism is to dissolve the hard shell of
unrecognized metaphysics which soon devitalizes science, to renew its
tender empiricism, and to set free philosophy and bring it in not as
doctrine but in the person of the philosopher, to take care of those
aspects of existence in the world which are of the greatest importance
but which are not fully reducible to objective knowledge.

III

The philosopher, then, concerned with these aspects of being which
are inaccessible to science, begins, like Descartes, with his own
existence, turns from the public external world to the private world
revealed to his own consciousness of himself; not, however, like
Descartes, because this gives him a foothold in immediate certainty
from which to walk out into the objective world, there is no continuity here with the objective world, but because here is the seat and
source of his own life. He finds here not objectivity but liberty, not
knowledge but choice: he stands before himself not as a reflective
intelligence but as an embodied person who must take up a position
and become something willed in relation to a definite situation. I
am 'a being who is not, but who can and ought to be'. I have to found
myself upon my own decisions consciously taken; and this is not an
act done once for all, but one that has to be sustained by being perpetually renewed so long as I live.

Self-consciousness when it is thoroughly awakened is consciousness of my solitude and my liberty. When everything goes of itself and
is taken for granted, in my early life of impulse, instinct, obedience
to duty, submission to authority, the objective world hides me from
myself. What am I? I cannot be wholly reduced to or identified with
my body, my role in society, my actions, nor even my character which
is manifested in all my aspects. At the bottom is my liberty, the source
of my possibilities, of what I will to be. Existence for me is this active
choice of myself in liberty. If I do not come to myself and exercise
my liberty in the realm of being-oneself, I remain in the realm of
being-there, objectively determined, a thing. When I do come to myself, accompanied by the anguish and the thrill of knowing that all

48

I think, decide, and do separates me from the solid ground of being-there, I launch myself in flight. The emptiness of liberty, the recognition that I cannot find myself in the objective aspects of my existence, that I am not an object but a possible existence (not an I-am but a what-am-I? which resolves into what-shall-I-be?), to which I am awakened and to which I perpetually return so long as I maintain myself at the level of being-oneself, is 'the consciousness of my essence'.

When with this consciousness of essence I found myself in decisions and commitments, my choice is existential and absolute; it cannot be reduced to psychological explanation in terms of motives, nor merely subsumed under a rational ethical principle: it is original, my choice of myself. To the self it has the sense of assurance, of inevitability: 'I come to myself as a gift: it is clear, it is evident, now that it is decided it can never be other than simple: how has it been possible for doubt to last so long!' This unconditioned affirmation of the self in decisions and choice which shatters all doubt seems to be a scandal from the point of view of philosophy. The difficulty is this: unless I have an original essence which has some positive content and is not empty liberty, how can I found myself in decisions which are self-determined; how can I know what I am in order to become what I am, unless I have a positive essence, that is to say, a nature? The answer seems to be that the choices I make and sustain and by which I make myself constitute the consistent ground of further spontaneous choice (not my nature, but my history). And beyond my first conscious decisions by which I constitute myself at the level of being-oneself, is an original self, obscure in origin but definite in actuality, rooted in a body and temperament and disposition and occupying a concrete situation in history, the self that exists at the level of being-there: this original self I cannot choose because it is given, but I can assume it, that is to say, adopt it as mine, as me. I who exist in liberty by conscious separation from my empirical self adopt all that which is uniquely mine 'as the manifested body of what I can be'. I identify myself with myself and face and acknowledge the vital impulses of the body, the brute facts of nature, the obligations of duty, the limitations of my situation and of all chosen ends: these enter into my decisions, but I am not subdued to them, am not a resultant of their determinations; these are the conditions and resistances which maintain me in the flight of liberty, if I have the skill and the will. But the flight can never be completely successful.

49

The fact that it is hampered can itself be interpreted. The effort at self-realization by its very frustration may bring about self-transcendence.

Therefore, although I have no essence, my situation is determined and my authentic choice is necessary. I come to myself as if I were a gift to myself, and I recognize that I have to realize my liberty in the world and to lose it in the Transcendence which is its ground and its limit, its source and its goal. This orientation towards Transcendence through the world is the general determination of my choice, within which my own personal uniqueness plays its part producing a choice which is marked by a wholly specific personal necessity—the sole criterion of the authenticity of my choice, objectively unverifiable—not physical, nor moral, nor logical. The self which I am invited to become is the self which I am in my situation, historical and transcendental. There is no alternative self; the only other alternatives are the failure to become myself and the refusal to be myself. This necessity does not do away with my liberty because it is not objective. On the one hand, it is my own personal uniqueness; on the other, it is my own faith in Transcendence—which can never be objectively secured, for, like Kierkegaard's, its very reality involves it in tension with its polar opposite. 'In not believing is belief. In belief is not believing . . . the force of belief is in the polarity'. Being-oneself turns on the poles of belief and unbelief.

'No choice without decision, no decision without will, no will without duty, no duty without being'; this formula shows choice proceeding from its source in myself, to which it also returns in making me become what I am. Such choice is no hopping uncertainty before alternatives; it is elicited from me, it proceeds straight to its goal. It is a disciplined choice: duty has a place in the series, not above but next below the source; I am not under the ethical law, I adopt the ethical law; in proceeding from liberty withdrawn to liberty engaged I accept determination by law, and if I set aside one law I appeal to another ('the only universal is the law of legality in general'). To look for a law is already to be free from the causal nexus, to be an origin, to be concerned for value in the concrete decision. The matured self in which the law has been assimilated and has fertilized experience is inventive and of higher validity than the objective law because more nearly total. Thus the self is put above the law, as indeed it is by Kant. But the self is not identified with the law, as in Kant, as the law of my nature, my rational essence. My essence is

50

liberty, I have no essence; that is the height and dizziness of my true position: suicide and defiance of the law are no less consistent with my essence than assimilation of the law and sensitively informed choice and activity. It is for me to say what I will be. My consciousness of myself as having to choose, without being able to escape the responsibility by recourse to any objective determinant of any kind, breaks the objective determination of me as being-there and constitutes me an unconditioned self. That is the summit of personal existence (being-oneself) to which I have constantly to return to renew the authenticity of myself in liberty.

[Existentialists are necessarily highly concerned with the subtle and complex relations between law and liberty, the objective norms of ethics and the subjective reality of the self and its exigencies. No simple statement of these relations is possible. Nietzsche is interested in the prolonged discipline of law as the indispensable means of maturing the vital grace of spontaneous movement in action and attitude, immediacy in choice and decision; but this appreciation of the pragmatic value of law in the history of cultures and the production of types is dominated by his sense of the crisis of values at this point in history. Jaspers, too, recognizes that mature choice presupposes an immense experience and that obedience is the leisurely childhood of liberty, but his conception both of the purgative value of law and of the ethical choice of the self is different. Submission to law is itself freedom in so far as it is a break with the unconscious determinants and a rise to the consciousness of value: but that puts all in question and leads on to choice. In choice, the self, knowing its liberty, its inescapable responsibility for itself, is not constrained by the law but adopts it in the given situation as the law of its own dispositions enabling it to become itself; the law is then a means, a mediation, explicative not reductive, maieutic not magisterial. In principle the law can only enlighten, never justify, the personal decision.]

IV

The consciousness of its liberty which awakens the self to personal existence in the realm of being-oneself is bound to a consciousness of itself as a self in the world, limited inescapably by its situation in the world, a situation which cannot be shared, which can only be known from within, and which, although it can be modified, cannot be changed into anything other than a situation in the world imposing narrow limits. I cannot change my parents or sex, nor my own past, nor altogether the fate and fortune of my lot in the world, but I can accept and adopt them and make them my own. This acceptance, my historicity, is more than resignation, as submission to law is more than obedience; it is affirmative and renewed and remains in constant tension with other possibilities: I am bound to my destiny and I love it as I love myself. My liberty so long as it refuses reality and remains for itself in the realm of possibility encounters no limits, but then I become nothing and am nothing; when it assumes the concrete embodied person I am in my situation in the world, it encounters limits which cannot in any way be got round, or reduced, or explained: they are simply there, and defy both comprehension and mastery. To recognize that these limits define the permanent impossibility of my realizing myself in the world is the necessary disillusion and despair on the further side of which is the possibility of self-transcendence, for then the limits are accepted as the end only for particular aims and forms of attachment and for the general understanding, and they may become frontiers where Transcendence is met. The perpetual temptation to escape from this situation in mysticism or positivism or intellectualism, to refuse to recognize that there is an irreducible duality between being-oneself and being-there in the world, that the authentic self which transcends the empirical world in liberty is doomed to frustration in the tasks and ends and ideals which it must nevertheless seriously engage in pursuing, as the only way of being-oneself and of reaching being-in-itself, this tension is the ethical situation at the heart of Jaspers's philosophy.

Ingredient in the concrete particular situation of every self are the inescapable limitations inherent in the human situation, such as death, suffering, conflict, fault. Human life in the world is riddled with the dreadful insecurity and irremediability of these universal limits. But it is not the taking note of them as objective facts that brings home their full fatality; it is only in the irreplaceable bitterness of personal experience of them in the pursuits in which we are engaged that personal existence may learn to accept them as definitive and at the same time find that they are not dead-ends but frontiers where being-in-itself is to be encountered. Death, for example, so long as I am forgetting it or fleeing from it or merely taking note of it as the inevitable end, is just an empirical fact about an empirical object in the world of being-there; it is not constitutive of my life, and in so far as it is not I am not living at the level of being-oneself. My death is present, it is constitutive of my relation to the phenomena in which my whole life is manifested: it puts in question the sense in which I am more than the phenomena of my objective appearance. When I lose a friend by death with whom I lived in communication, the communication is struck but the presence of the lost one is not wholly destroyed, and by my fidelity is maintained and continues to influence me. Thus death institutes a test, and becomes a sieve: does the essential survive? There is no objective test, the answer lies with me. If I fear that nothing can survive this test, perhaps it is because I have not yet fully come to myself in liberty but am still immersed in the world of calculations. Indeed that is more to be feared than death, the loss of oneself which comes from attachment to objective substitutes (for example, a party or the State) or by falling back into being-there, so that one dies without having lived. If I become myself, even though I can have no reasonable hope whatever of my survival in any form linked in continuity of memory with my present self, so that there can be no other world for me that is not this world, nevertheless I can both will to realize myself in this world without losing myself in the world and will my death as my natural consummation without seeking refuge in it. In such ways, death is not a mere limit but a clue and a proof. Neither can I separate myself, at the level of being-oneself, from suffering; for there is always the suffering of others, and mere happiness is a kind of sleep in which we are not conscious of true being. Conflict and violence are inextricably woven into the texture of human culture. I have to consent to them if I participate in the life of the world. There is no absolute decision on principle which will absolve me from having to choose between violence and submission in each actual situation, although I know that neither the one nor the other can ever bring universal or final justice, peace, and harmony. But it is in the non-violent striving with others for authentic personal existence that the limit is most sharply disclosed and I am laid open to all possibilities, for it is an ardent strife, suspicious of all sentimentality and pity and complacency, vigilant against the tendency to dominate or to submit, concerned to put everything in question in oneself and in the other, to dissolve every crystallization, to break up every acquisition, to remit every conclusion. Lastly, in Jaspers's view imperfection, failure, fault inhere in the human situation as fatally as death, suffering, and conflict. Not only is there in the human depths a destructive element, morbid or wild, but also success is never more than partial, in doing good I indirectly do evil, my own good profits by the evil which others have done, and my choice of myself in liberty is itself necessarily tainted in both attitude and content (for it is self-assertion and pride, which is the source of conflict, and it is made good in the adoption of an actual self and a concrete situation riddled with imperfections, and issues in decisions which can only be decisions at the cost of some impurity of motive and some arbitrariness of judgement). The only purity I can have in the world is to recognize to the full my guilt and responsibility and to take it upon myself with an active conscience.

Such general limitations together with my own particular limitations are the material out of which I have to make my life; they can be partially overcome by being actively accepted and used, but they are real checks and frustrations and bring it home to me that neither can I realize myself in this world nor can the absolute reality I seek, being-in-itself, be found objectively realized in this world: that indeed, although it can only be known in this world, it is not this world. However, although it is true that if these limits, or some of them, are treated as vincible (utopianism) or as dead-ends (positivism) the human situation is falsified, nevertheless to take them as frontiers across which there is a right of entry into being-in-itself is no less a falsification. The encounter with Transcendence cannot be guaranteed. Positivism is only false in so far as it closes the frontier.

Thus the social ideal of human well-being completely and finally established, long and happy life without pain or privation, is dubious even as an ideal. Nietzsche was afraid that it was practicable, that modern ideas and technical success meant just this, and threatened to reduce mankind to a common level of green-meadow gregariousness, contentment, ease, security, and bovine mediocrity. Jaspers sees plainly enough the irregularity and intractibility of life which defies any such smooth reduction to control and ever threatens catastrophe, and he is therefore able to accept the aim of social well-being as valid for social policy and therefore for individual effort, so long as the dangerous depersonalizing tendencies of the present age of masses and machines and total planning are kept in mind and fought against.

In any case, the State stands for more than mere economic well-being. The State is the most formidable of all the objectivities which are indispensable but which enclose personal existence with the threat of lifeless emptiness. Because of its authority and power, as collective will manifesting the character of personal will with greater majesty, because of its appeal to the imagination with the call to great tasks and high destiny, because of its identification with duty and high ideals and the sweets of virtue, shaming the private desires of the heart, its claim to transcend its members as a system transcends its elements (which reverses the truth) is hard to resist. The individual has somehow to come to terms with the State, to find his vocation and his destiny within it, and to find in himself the source of criticism of its aims and ideals and its actual policies. The validity of the State is not a prior and overriding validity. As in the theoretical field the law can only enlighten, never justify, the personal decision, so in the practical field the State can never give meaning and value to personal existence but only stimulus, scope, and opportunity. The individual needs the State for becoming himself, and the State derives its validity from being-oneself; but there is tension as well as fertility in the relation. The State mediates the participation of the person in history, in the total human tradition. The individual does not get the meaning of his life from history, there is no philosophy of history; nevertheless, his life and activity have to make sense in the historical context, have to participate in the continuity of man's life. History is open, and the written record is not the last word. Even the authority of success, upheld by the finality of the past, cannot prevent the submerged possibilities from coming to the surface, from influencing the future.

Thus it is always necessary for being-oneself to assimilate the objectivity which it actively accepts; and this is what gives meaning and value to social policies and institutions and to the course of history. Being-oneself, which would stand aside from the empirical world, being-there, or remain in the margin, is sterile and self-destructive. But a happy marriage of the two is not always, perhaps never, possible. The heretic and the rebel warn us, exceptions though they are, of what the world is like, of what is possible and may be necessary. Nietzsche's *amor fati*, embracing our destiny, the existentialist's commitment and fidelity when he assumes his own parents and his own past, his personal situation and human life in the world, and remains ever active and creative, although perforce patient and checked, this being-oneself, my historicity, is real because the other possibilities remain open, of which the mystic and the suicide are reminders. In such a world, which must be both accepted and refused, personal existence, being-oneself, can only be lived in the spirit of irony, humour, and modesty. The objective world, being-there, is not being-in-itself, the ultimate reality; but this reality is not to be looked for anywhere else, nor need it be abandoned as a hopeless quest. It is not revealed to consciousness in general, the universal subject to whom the public objective world is scientifically intelligible, nor is it revealed to pure subjectivity cultivating states of mind: it is revealed to the embodied subject who wills his relations with an objective world with the intention to transcend both subject and object, to gain in relation to being-there the transcendence of being-oneself and being-in-itself. This consciousness is modest because it is rare, playful and ironic because it sees that the world must be taken very seriously and its pretensions not too seriously. Neither idealism nor scientific rationalism has this humour, for want of having broken the pretensions of the objective world. On the other hand, the irony of the existentialist is not the mockery of the sceptic nor the amusement of the spectator, for he suffers from the frustrations of this world and loves and seeks the being-in-itself which is hidden in its appearances.

To take one's stand in the veritable human situation is to engage oneself in the tasks and pursuits of life in the world without illusion, taking upon oneself death, suffering, conflict, fault as bonds and bounds; and at the same time to go forward as if in the promise of having life abundantly. To disengage oneself (for example, as a spectator or mystic) is not to raise oneself above the world but to fail to become oneself. To engage oneself blindly or without detachment (as in utopianism or hedonism) is to remain sunk in the empirical world of being-there. Philosophy which opens man's eyes to his condition and exposes him to the temptation of despair, also brings him the faith by which he goes on.

V

My being awakened to liberty and self-choice, unconditioned being-oneself, is the doing of another, like Christian salvation. In any case, my unconditioned self is oriented towards other unconditioned selves, requires and seeks communication with them: my uniqueness is elicited by and requires the uniqueness of others, and is otherwise unthinkable. Being-oneself is not real without communication, just as empty liberty is not real without manifesting itself in choice. My liberty posits and requires the liberty of everybody else. The formula is: 'I will that each other shall be what I strive to become, that he be himself in sincerity and in truth'. This appeal to the other is accompanied by self-revelation without reserve; one dares 'to be naked' before the other: the formalities, conventions, and reserves of ordinary intercourse are inappropriate to communication at the level of being-oneself. One becomes oneself and brings the other to himself in thus opening oneself to him. For this communication is not the sharing of what is in common but insistence upon the authentic singularity of each. It is therefore conflict, but a 'loving struggle', the struggle of beings who recognize themselves as united but have as a condition of their reality to assert and maintain their difference and to question and challenge themselves and each other. The truth of each is the truth of himself and for him there is no alternative, his uniqueness is a vital assimilation and affirmation which is his alone: there is no other truth, but there is the truth of others. The 'loving struggle' of communication is the corrective of the unavoidable arbitrariness in this necessary solitude of truth. Existences are linked by reason and in communication strive to bring themselves to the unity which they have by faith. The separation is never wholly overcome: truth remains invincibly multiple, a conflict of absolutes not a totality of perspectives, a call to being-oneself and to communication not a form of knowledge, for the total object of knowledge is lost in Transcendence which cannot be apprehended in its unity. Here again, therefore, there is frustration; but no relaxation of the effort to communicate. Communication is between persons who participate in a common world order and collaborate in common tasks which humanize relations between individuals, but communication does not reside in this intercourse, it springs from it. The other is properly constituted for me as a person by my being fully myself, that is, communication is in the world of being-oneself. Otherwise, he is another one like me and all others, an object and a means, a figure in the world, a rational consciousness equivalent with every other, and one who interests me only in so far as we envisage a common object or form a common thought universally valid or participate in a common society. This objectification of communication is like the objectification which reduces the 'thou' to a 'he'; it forms the substratum from which true communication may rise and to which it may sink. Love, 'the absolute consciousness in its plenitude', is always possible, and always desired by the person awakened to being-oneself. Ideas which claim objective validity pass away, but 'there are always the men with whom I am or can be in communication, and with them what is for me authentic being stands firm'. Communication is not limited to contemporaries physically encountered; it is possible to seek and to touch authentic being-oneself in history, not necessarily the men of external greatness and success, but the men of faith, love, and imagination who move and call me to become myself.

Communication, the most essential of existential tasks, is the most precious and the most fragile of all possible achievements.

VI

Being-there (the objective world known by observation and experiment), being-oneself (the personal existence of one who is awakened to his liberty and assumes his historicity and affirms himself in decision and choice), being-in-itself (the Transcendence of the world, manifested in the world and inseparable from it), these three realms of Being are in no sense reducible to one another. The person who is made aware of them may participate in all three; Transcendence embraces the world of objects and subjects: but the logical understanding, formed upon the objects of empirical existence, being-there, is unable without falsification to describe the other realms of existence or to bring them into a common system; their discontinuity is invincible, only to be reconciled in the life of a person and by faith in Transcendence. Philosophy can no longer naïvely attempt to treat the whole of Being as immanent in the logical understanding. Reason can attempt to clarify and fortify personal existence, being-oneself, and to awaken it in others; and to awaken philosophic faith in Transcendence and to guide the perception of it. The whole effort of philosophy is to bring me to the presence and the silence of Transcendence, only accessible from the level of being-oneself. Indeed, being-oneself is, so to speak, itself only the place where one listens to the voice and the silence of Transcendence, a voice which speaks only riddles, a presence which is sometimes a plenitude and often a lack. The riddles can never be made plain to universal understanding; each personal existence can only read them for itself, and only for the moment, perpetually, never once for all. Faith never becomes certainty, but the impulse to transcend is invincible; reason can never forsake the quest for unity and totality and never find them save in

Transcendence; personal existence can only be satisfied with absolute existence, being-oneself with being-in-itself.

I am autonomous but not self-sufficient: I become what I am. In the dizzy consciousness of myself in liberty, I lean not only upon my actual situation in the world imposing its limits but also upon the Transcendence before which I stand; I stand in consciousness of my liberty before my concrete situation and before the enveloping situation which gives me my responsibility, my liberty: I am unconditioned, in my liberty, and doubly dependent. I actively accept my situation in the world and strive to transcend it, the objects before me, the limited ends I adopt, the hindrances to my will, and all ultimate frustrations. I will myself, and am in that sense my origin; at the same time, I am given to myself, for I am, so to speak, commissioned to will myself, liberty is my situation in which I find myself, and that unconditioned self to which I return and in which I renew myself is my transcendence and my link with the Transcendence of the world as the ground of my being. Personal existence, being-oneself, which we can be, is one with Transcendence, being-in-itself, through which we are. When personal existence becomes sure of itself it becomes in the same operation sure of Transcendence. The unconditioned I, freed from determinations, standing in liberty, knows that I am autonomous but not self-sufficient, that I am doubly dependent, given to myself from a transcendental ground and in need of the limitations and determinations by which I choose myself, realize myself in the world.

My authenticity is in this autonomy, doubly dependent. There is no place in this philosophy for mysticism, for separation from the world and direct communication with God. If the term God (which savours of myth) is to be used, there is no God apart from the world, nor is the world God: God is both revealed and hidden in the world, and no effort to see his face can be finally successful nor finally baffled. One might perhaps say that the condition of looking steadfastly upon his face is continually to lose sight of it. Life is like that: its vitality withers unless it is perpetually renewed, and so soon as it is seized in one form it slips into another, even the opposite; so that paradox is the least inadequate formulation. Nothing is safe, once for all. The Transcendence of the world, the meaning of life, is found alike in frustration and failure and in consummate achievement; but it is not either, and it is not found in either if they remain what they are and are not cancelled and transcended, without any final escape from the situation in which achievement is real and must be attempted, and frustration is bitter, and failure a grief and a crisis to be dealt with. There is no respite from this tension of unconditioned action in the world, springing from myself in liberty and moving across the world to its limits, at any point or moment meeting the tangent of Transcendence, and striving to hold in steady contemplation the unity and transfiguration of the world.

Jaspers seeks to give to this refractory but veridical experience the clarification and formal validity of rigorous philosophical treatment, following through the thought in all its intricacy and ramification. The main phase of this treatment is the development of a doctrine of ciphers. The world is, so to speak, a secret text which can never be translated into public language. It is only intelligible to personal existence and can only be deciphered by each for himself. 'I live with the ciphers. I do not understand them but I steep myself in them. All their truth lies in the concrete intuition which fills them in a manner each time historical.' The entire vast panorama of nature and history is at this point embraced by Jaspers's philosophy, for nothing is indifferent, there is nothing which may not in a favourable moment give this intuition of Transcendence. Nevertheless, philosophy can help to make it easier, can elaborate a new objectivity, a second universe of objects which will indicate and illustrate the general truth of human experience. Such a task can only be tentative, and would mislead if it pretended to any precision of doctrine or method, for there is nothing which cannot be a cipher, and there can be no settled meaning for any; there is no code and no key. Nonetheless, the general experience of mankind has a testimony which reports on the enigmatical world, and this witness can be examined and interpreted for what it is worth. This testimony is given mainly in myths and religions and philosophies. They are not so much true as ciphers revealing the truth, not universal truth but special appropriations of the truth. Therefore the approach to them for this purpose is at the level of communication, not by the objective method of sociological classification. From the standpoint of philosophy, it is especially the history of philosophy that reveals Transcendence and leads to the orientation of the present effort in philosophy: it is a ceaseless communication of the living philosopher with the philosophers of the past, who are thinkers living their lives and thinking in order to live well, not anonymous workers whose production is capitalized in results.

Myths, religions, and philosophies are commentaries, ciphers at one remove from the original ciphers of nature and history and personal existence. The amazing exuberance and monstrous incoherence of nature, its numberless faces, make it the most fertile source of ciphers. In poetry and in painting the natural world is often treated as a cipher, the indication of something other than itself. Jaspers gives the example of Van Gogh for this use of the imagination to invoke a world beyond the world of appearances but manifested in it. The poetic and the scientific treatment of nature may be profoundly philosophical, whereas the attempts at definitive readings of nature in philosophies of nature are unphilosophical, in the sense of pretending to give a knowledge which is not knowledge, and not a cipher. Similarly, the philosophies of history which give a definitive reading of man's destiny are unphilosophical, whereas a reading of history which does not make a principle of success, but explores other possibilities and keeps the future open and seeks to touch in history the secret and authentic life of personal existence and to follow its vicissitudes, is philosophical and finds in history a cipher revealing Transcendence. The cipher *par excellence* is personal existence, for here in my finite self-determination in individual choice and decisions is the conjunction of nature and history in a microcosm. My liberty realized in my life in the world is the formula by which I read from within Transcendence in the world. But it is not the success, the happy realization of this union which I manifest in my effort at self-realization that reveals Transcendence; it is the reality of it, the perpetual possibility and the perpetual frustration. Being-in-itself which is the meaning of this world is touched at the limits of positive action and communication in this world, at the points of frustration in which all our human pursuits and efforts culminate. But is it indeed absolute being which is touched at these points, or is it absolute nothingness? 'Only silence remains possible in face of the silence which is in the world.' Anguish, patience, and peace are indissolubly linked in this experience of the empirical world, for the ruin is real but is not for certain the last word. Ultimate frustration is a cipher which cannot be interpreted: it is silence. There can only be faith in being-in-itself which sustains and orients the effort of being-oneself and this faith is touched and tested at the limits of achievement and failure. The final word can never be said in any shape or form, and therefore the task remains and is worth while, and philosophy can point the way and save one from a failure of nerve.

The three orders of being limit, break, and interpret one another, and the fatal error is to take any one of them exclusively: each is irremediably false save in tension with the others. That is the clue to philosophy and to life. In Jaspers himself, the finality of self-affirmation (final only in recurrence), bruised and knocked back, is unqualified affirmation of Being, *amor fati*, embraced with the highest intensity of imagination and will.

VII

Jaspers's philosophy is not a natural theology, but it might be said that it takes the place of a natural theology. It is not a Christian philosophy, but it is dealing philosophically with the elusive realities dealt with cryptically in the sayings of Jesus. Jaspers's notion of Transcendence is not theistic, neither is it pantheistic. At the same time, it is not naturalistic nor anthropocentric. He explicitly, emphatically, and uncompromisingly rejects both religion and atheism. He rejects religion because it claims to be authoritative and undertakes to guarantee and to administer the experience of Transcendence, and because it stands for a beyond which is another world, not a beyond which is the upshot, the hidden meaning, of this world, which can only be known out of and by means of the plenitude and deficiencies of life in the world. For Jaspers, Transcendence is a total view of the world, not from the station of Sirius as a spectator of all time and all existence, but by glimpses gained through participation in the life of the world by one who is eager to see and trained to look. Anything approaching separation from the world or the treatment of anything in the world as sacred or privileged is peremptorily rejected. At the same time, atheistic positivism is rejected because it denies the possibility of Transcendence, and because it proceeds to find substitutes which are too obviously faked. His criticism of Nietzsche is here much to the point. How shall one interpret the ultimate frustration which being-oneself encounters in the world? The option lies between despair, life in the world is not really possible, and the treatment of frustration as revealing the hidden secret of the world, and this option is only kept open by the possibility of faith in Transcendence which is inspired by irrecusable elements of our experience which the ciphers and our own will to affirm help us to interpret. The will to affirm, even in the acceptance of final frustration, is essential, although it cannot subsist on itself without the encouragement of real experiences. Nietzsche carries his nihilism to the extreme, says No to all that is accepted and valued, not wantonly but because he has to, but he does it in order really to be able to say Yes to existence with sincerity and assurance. But the terms in which he finds himself able to say Yes are puerile, crude notions taken from science, pseudo-science, and primitive metaphysics, to fake an atheist's Transcendence. Better, and unavoidable, the silence of Transcendence, the riddle of the ciphers. Thus Jaspers explicitly rejects idealism and positivism, revealed religion and atheism, materialism and hedonism; and at the same time finds a place and a partial justification for them all. The final word between them is not said and cannot be said. There is no trace of agnosticism here, however, for that also is a point of view which is confined to the level of being-there; he takes up an uncompromising position on the level of being-oneself, one that is bound to give offence to all parties.

Jaspers tries to bring his ship safely through Scylla and Charybdis, Kierkegaard and Nietzsche, and we seem to find him cast first upon one and then upon the other. The obvious criticism is that in choosing this passage he has doomed himself to founder; in particular, that his philosophic faith in Transcendence is an impotent substitute for Christian faith in the God of salvation, which in the ruined world which he gives us is a poor sort of joke. This criticism is far too easy, but his notion of Transcendence inevitably invites comparison with the God of theology and raises the question whether his interpretation of experience is not too deeply informed by Christian conceptions to be capable of inspiring a positive humanism. Thus, in spite of himself, he gets pushed into the position of a natural theology, like the alliance of Christian modernism with some form of Platonic or Hegelian idealism, positions which have proved unstable and provoke a return to Christian doctrine or the passage to atheism, which is to be cast upon Kierkegaard or upon Nietzsche. Nevertheless, it is a mistake to think that Jaspers is really open to this kind of criticism, not merely because his own *amor fati* is so different from Nietzsche's embrace of the world and his own philosophic faith so different from Kierkegaard's longing for eternity, but because his philosophy is existential, that is to say, an invitation to experience and a clue to experience, not a description of Being. The philosophy of existence effaces itself in the irreplaceable experience of a personal existence: all lines lead into this, and there is no independent picture or diagram;

that is why so many of the strokes of doctrine efface each other, lest any construction emerge which can satisfy the mind and prove a substitute for personal existence. Taken otherwise, the philosophy is too baffling for anyone's patience, since it is built upon its own undoing: the confident prescription based upon faith in Transcendence which is the philosophy is shadowed by the unremitting insistence that it is all in question. But the effort of the whole enterprise is to light up personal existence, not to build an argument. Kierkegaard's tension between belief and unbelief, in which his life is suspended, is used by Jaspers to precipitate personal existence into experience of Transcendence. The existentialist refusal to objectify truth which Kierkegaard uses to reawaken Christians to the meaning of their faith, Jaspers uses to initiate and control a fruitful experience of the empirical world. Faithful to this existential method, he deals no less faithfully with the broadest aspects and the subtlest reaches of human experience in the world, maintaining throughout with rigour the standards of modern technical philosophy. His impressive achievement must leave its mark on philosophy.

But if the effort of Jaspers's philosophy is to promote personal encounters with Transcendence, surely the experience can give some account of itself? 'One does not prove Transcendence, one bears witness to it.' His work of course does abound in indications of this experience. Consider some of the many ways in which we do experience not Transcendence but transcendence, in the sense of something which is not in the actual situation but which the situation invokes and which in some sense completes it. The psychological tension of urgent situations, as in tragedy, moves us with a sense of implication: What is true that this can be possible? Jaspers says, generalizing this consciousness, 'Being is such that this empirical world is possible'. Reading the cipher thus, although it does not immediately lead to any intuitive perception of the nature of Being, is better than a deceptive satisfaction with some discursive rationalist explanation. In this way literature is a cipher, for it creates heightened situations which wring their implications from the responsive mind. Similarly, it is defect and deficiency that occasion ideals: justice is a cry. No achievement is once for all: histories and biographies are never final and never superseded; themes may become hackneyed but can never be exhausted; on the one hand, life is ever the same, on the other, it requires perpetual renewal. Everything actual, every realization, can never be more than a participation, pointing beyond itself. Thus life itself, in the stoic conception, can be played as a game, in which the content is indifferent, the style is all.

When Jaspers takes as the chief cipher personal existence, a microcosm, transcending the empirical world and itself requiring and pointing to Transcendence, whether he is justified or not, he is anyhow speaking out of a full experience in a world which is alive with transcendence, and in which that fact is a way of life and a source of hope for many who cannot respond to the witness of his faith. At any rate, the strenuousness of Jaspers's own faith compels respect: it is neither a formula nor an indolent disinclination to count on the calculable; as with a wrestler, the issue is always uncertain, and everything may turn on the tension of the moment. It is not in the spirit of a torturer that he screws up the tensions (as perhaps it is with Kierkegaard), but rather with the technical precision of a gymnast training for a specific achievement. There are certain tensions, polarities, relativities by which the precious and precarious personal existence is kept in good form. It is the tension of infinite alertness for the undreamed of that braces his pursuit of the vision of Transcendence. In this pursuit there can be no rules and techniques to relieve the strain. There can be no question here of easy faith, what is in question is whether or not the fine edge is brittle, the elasticity overstretched. To quit metaphors, perhaps misleading, for the dominant impression Jaspers leaves is of the heroic intensity of an impassioned intelligence for whom the tensions are real but dynamic and endurable, even if his doctrine founders as a philosophy it succeeds as philosophy, as the vehicle of a movement of thought which is a man's life and carries essential recognitions able to inspire and enlighten new initiatives in the effort both to think and to live.

IV

GABRIEL MARCEL

(Born 1889)

*agnostic converted
to Catholicism
viz Mauriac*

I

THE thought of Gabriel Marcel is even less susceptible of summary treatment than that of Jaspers, with which it has close affinities. His philosophy is a philosophy of second thoughts, a reflection upon reflection, not raising reflection to a higher degree of abstraction but using reflection to restore concreteness, the unity of living and thinking. The method congenial to him is to note in a journal his trains of thought, which exposes the intimate process of thinking, with all its hesitations and audacities, its tentatives and discontinuities, its polished fragments, suggestive beginnings, sudden triumphs, and abandoned pursuits. This is at the furthest remove from system building, and far even from systematic exposition. But the current of his thought does not run in the channel of daily occurrence (as with Amiel, for example), for it is strictly governed by certain dominant concerns; his thinking is neither mere philosophizing nor a philosophy, it is an act of philosophy, *la pensée pensante* not *la pensée pensée*. His repudiation of systems and results, the return to concreteness, was the fruit of his own slow-maturing philosophical development, which owed nothing to the influence of other existentialist thinkers; his acknowledged affinities with these thinkers are an outcome of the course which he was compelled to follow by the exigencies of his own thinking from an independent starting-point. He thought his way through Idealism and freed himself from its

66

spell, because he found that it denatured man and the world. The concern of his philosophy is to restore and explore the veridical and vital experiences which spring from man and the world in the plenitude of their being and the responsiveness of their encounter.

Like Jaspers, Marcel would bring philosophy back to the contemplation of Being. This supreme interest of classical philosophy has been destroyed by the Kantian and Bergsonian critiques, which in their different ways have lowered the status of the object to which we have intellectual access, and by the materialism of modern science and the contemporary preoccupation with technical knowledge for the sake of power. These developments stand as permanent and forbid any simple return to an Aristotelian metaphysics with its intellectual conception of Being in terms of grammar and logic. To reduce myself to thought in general and the objective world to a collection of universal characters is not the way to penetrate into the nature of things. But the alternative is not agnosticism nor scepticism. The first step is to retrace the steps which have been taken in abstract thought, to return to the unity of concrete being. The secrets of a world which is beyond object and subject yet the product of an active relation between them cannot be made an object of universal knowledge, immediately cognizable, a piece of intellectual public property.

Jaspers said of the *Cogito* of Descartes, as the starting-point of modern philosophy, that it was methodological not radical; it put in question the existence of the object of knowledge in order to show how that might be recovered and assured, but failed to call in question the form of being enjoyed by the knowing subject, to raise the question of my own being, what am I? Marcel, too, says that to be a subject is not a given fact for a point of departure, but an achievement and an end; by which he means, with all existentialists, that the knowing subject who apprehends the public object of knowledge is in practice a specialized function of the whole man, and in theory an abstraction from the human situation, and must not be mistaken for the existing individual (infinitely interested in existing, as Kierkegaard put it, and therefore intermittently interested in thinking) with whom philosophy is properly concerned. But Marcel is not so resolved as Jaspers to throw the whole weight of emphasis on the moment of withdrawal, the self-origination of the individual in liberty, the completion of the preliminary movement of Descartes; his accent stresses participation not self-affirmation, because, in a reflection as rigorous as it can be made upon the most intensely lived experiences, re-living them in reflective examination, he seeks a concrete philosophy which will introduce a current of air again into certain torpid regions of the spirit which modern habits of thought have closed up. Therefore he does not begin with a movement of withdrawal, like Descartes and Jaspers, but with a movement of return, a return to the body and to broken moorings. The thought of Descartes possesses itself but not its object, it is not in touch with anything—and that is a summing-up of Marcel's whole case against Idealism, indicating its failure to effect a real exchange with the object of thought, because a presence, a plenitude with which one is in responsive touch, cannot be thought, neither at the bottom of the scale in the commerce of the body with the environment in which it is inserted nor at the top in the communication between I and thou. His philosophy turns upon the poles of incarnation and invocation.

'The essence of man is to be in a situation.' Marcel, then, discovers man first as embedded in his concrete situation in the world, not in the moment of his separation from himself in the consciousness of his liberty. My awareness of my existence is not first of all a separation of myself as a knowing subject from my body as a known object, because it is the existence of my body in the world that constitutes me a subject before it is given to me as an object to a subject. This primordial participation of my bodily existence in the life of the world, in which I have a confused consciousness of universal existence before I come to separate awareness of my own existence, is lost to the first reflective consciousness which has established philosophy, but it can be restored by a second effort of thought which thus cancels the problem raised by the separation of thought from its object in reflective consciousness. Then the task of philosophy is to get rid of the false problems which arise from the first movement of reflection (and which fatally detain thought in permanent estrangement from experience, self-enclosed in a teasing maze from which there is no issue), and to institute a second movement of reflection which reinstates and re-lives essential experiences. The first of these is my experience of incarnation in a body which exists in continuity with all other objects in the world. But how am I related to my body, is that not a problem?

The immense majority of philosophers of all schools have thought so, but the relation depends in some sense on me, on my response to the original question, what am I? I can live in such a way that I belong to my body, am identified with it; or I can treat my body as an instrument in such a way that I am enslaved by it; for example, suicide is the extreme case in which I seem to dispose of my body with absolute freedom of choice, but in which I am really the victim of a tragic illusion, for the positive meaning of my liberty is the possibility of affirmation, the response to an invitation. Thus the I cannot adjudicate impersonally on the problem before me, because I am personally involved in it, I am myself in question with the question raised. In general, if I put in question my own total existence (what am I?) I cannot tackle the problem without presupposing the I which is called in question: in attempting to deal with it I am already affirming myself, not by saying so but by being; I am not saying something about myself but am the source of whatever can be said. Being is primary and present; knowledge is secondary and cannot prove Being or explain it, for knowledge works within an affirmation of Being and cannot but presuppose it. My own being, then, and the being in which I participate are not problems before me on which I can get to work, for I have no standing and no possible existence outside of Being, and the independent standing which seems to be given to the knowing subject in reflective consciousness is a mistake which further reflection corrects. This second reflection exercised in self-recollection, the moment of withdrawal (Jaspers's liberty) in which I separate and collect myself and take my stand over against my life, brings me an assurance of Being and a disposition of openness and permeability (Jaspers's personal existence sure of itself and in the same operation sure of Transcendence). *Being as mystery*

This learning to regard Being not as a problem but as a mystery is fundamental in Marcel. His distinction between a mystery and a problem, he insists, is capital. A mystery, in his sense, is not a problem which lies beyond the scope of present knowledge; it is an experience which is quite indubitable and which escapes in principle being reduced to a public object before a universal subject: subject and object interpenetrate and cannot be separated; they are mutually involved constituents each of the other. He gives many examples in addition to the question of Being, the ontological mystery. For instance, the problem of evil cannot be dealt with as a problem because the question, Why is there evil, death, etc., itself takes away the possibility of an answer. For if the evil is explained, there is no evil and no question; but it continues to touch me; I am involved, and for me it cannot be reduced to anything other than it is: it cannot appropriately be dealt with by assigning a cause nor by constructing an ideal world; it is ultimate, not problematic. Or love, reduced to concepts or primitive elements in the Freudian or other psychological analysis, remains what it is in personal experience. In this way, being, evil, love, freedom, and many other such realities of which we have vital assurance, are falsified by treatment as objective problems; and unless reflection returns upon itself and re-opens immediate approach to these concrete experiences, our habits of thought forbid our entry into the most habitable regions in which we are most truly at home and ourselves. The work of philosophy, by this second movement of reflection, is to release spontaneous recognitions and responses which the first reflective movement of scientific culture has inhibited. The positive immediacy of human being is under duress, and it is the work of reason to set it free and to restore its confidence. Marcel's doctrine of mystery, like Plato's myth of anamnesis, is the recovery by learning of a lost privileged immediacy: when we have learned to think away what we have learned to think, we are again in touch with what we had lost, and further thinking then reveals it to us. The assurance of my own being which I can gain in this way, of the I which transcends my body and my life, is not ever compulsory, in the way in which a deduction in logic may be necessary. I can regard myself as nothing but my own body. I can despair. I can end my life. Indeed, the world of experience is a standing and pressing invitation to deny or ignore my transcendence. The logical understanding developed in the first phase of reflection instigates doubt and denial. The assurance of Being restored by a concrete philosophy in the second phase of reflection, defining the status and competence of knowledge (within and not outside, responsive to and not master of, the enfolding and primary mystery of Being), is only the first step; but thereafter the way lies open to an exploration of Being by reflection upon certain intensely lived experiences, viz., fidelity, hope, love, which are indubitable and revealing.

II

Before turning to these experiences, consider the pivotal distinction between what I am and what I have. What I have is external to me and independent of me. I dispose of it in some sense, have powers over it. Is my body something which I have in this way? The issue is

70

seen in a crucial case in suicide, which is the disposal of a life by the owner. But how is the owner really related to the life he disposes of? Suppose a person feels he has no right to dispose of his own life? What is this I which disposes or refuses to dispose of a life? The I is, so to speak, defined by its liberty, the possibility in the face of life to accept or to refuse it. This is the primary subject-object relation. This liberty is permanent: despair is always possible, an open invitation. The power to dispose of which inheres in having separates the I from what it has and puts it on a higher plane: they are not on the same footing in a reciprocal relationship. The verb to have is seldom used in the passive voice; the active passage from subject to object is irreversible. These are indications of the I as being, involved in the I as having.

To have is to have the power to keep to oneself or to give up, and to exhibit to another, or to oneself as another. Thus to have implies another, if only oneself considered as another. Even my opinions are my own because I have first had the opinions of others and have rejected them. In all having, even the most completely intimate possession of properties (attributes), there is a tension between interior and exterior. Properties are powers efficacious in the outside world. Possession of an exterior object involves the I in anxieties. Even where there is lack of possession, mere desire is a form of having, and this desire to enjoy possession corresponds to the anxiety about losing what is possessed.

In spite of the higher plane on which the I stands in having, so that I dispose of what I have and am not disposed of, I cannot dispose of the relation of having, and am affected by it. The verb to have has its full force in the active voice, but has a common and significant meaning in the passive. One thinks to have, and is had; had literally and also in the sense of being deceived in thinking only to have. This is especially true of the body. ' It seems indeed to be the essence of my body or of my tools in so far as I treat them as possessed, to tend to suppress me, me who possesses them.' This is least true when we are working creatively on the material we have, as the musician with his instrument, the scientist with his apparatus, the gardener with his plot and his plants. The reverse is then nearer the truth: being is not reduced to having, but having is transformed into being. This abolishes the duality and the tension between interior and exterior, between what I am and what I have. When my ideas most resemble inert possessions securely mine, I am myself most possessed by them, most a fanatic under their tyranny. The genuine thinker remains creative because his thought is always being put in question and put to the test. Both he and his ideas are alive and assimilated to each other.

Thus to live on the level of having (or desiring to have) is to lose the height proper to the position of the I, to abandon what I am and become what I have, to be reduced to a thing. On the other hand, the I cannot stand aloof on its superior level, drawing to its most tenuous thread its connection with the world of having, as in the ascetic practices of the East. Marcel says, with an impulse of unusual violence:

'My most intimate and unshakable conviction—and if it is heretical so much the worse for orthodoxy—is, whatever so many of the pious and learned people may have said about it, that God does not at all want to be loved by us over *against* the created, but to be glorified through the created and starting from it. That is why so many pious books are intolerable to me. This God standing against the created and in some way jealous of his own works is in my eyes nothing but an idol. It is an escape for me to have written this. And I declare till a new dispensation that I shall be insincere each time that I shall seem to affirm anything contrary to what I have just written.' (*Être et Avoir*, pp. 196–7.)

The world has been denatured and profaned by Christian and secularist alike, for their different reasons, and it is the effort of Marcel's philosophy to restore 'a reverential love of the created' as the condition both of humanism and of the possibility of again hearing the Christian message. His Christianity is first and last a Christian humanism. Apart from the question of faith, is the metaphysical mystery of existence, which is not to be explored beyond the world of having but lies in the mid-region between having and being, between me and my life, between the self and the world, a region in which the self opens itself to the world and unfolds and is transcended in a participation which is its subjective reality. The body is the kernel or the symbol of this middle region when we do not treat it as an independent reality closed upon itself, but rather as an outcrop of a submerged kingdom whose main extent lies below the surface of the water.

'The very fact of living, in the full meaning which we give to the word when we speak of our life, of human life, would it not imply, for anyone whose thought would penetrate to the bottom of it, the existence of a kind of metaphysical Atlantis, inexplorable by definition, but whose presence in reality confers on our experience its volume, its value, its mysterious density?' (*Du Refus à l'Invocation*, p. 124.)

Thus the tension between being and having, what I am and what I have, is normal and necessary, is the very plot of the drama, and every attempt to abolish it by reduction to having or by elimination of having (that is, in the most typical forms of materialism, idealism, and theology) brings down the curtain. Life is achieved by resolving the tension in responsive feeling and creative activity, in which having is not eliminated but is assimilated to being, in which one and another become I and thou; in which science is integrated with metaphysics; in which autonomy ('managing my own affairs') is transcended in liberty, which is participation; in which my body and the world with which it is consubstantial and which enlarges and multiplies its powers is the place in which I bear witness to Being; in which I work out my fidelity and my hope and keep myself open, fluid, and ready to spend (*disponible*).

This theme is paralleled in the realm of perception and cognition. Marcel having proved for himself the inadequacy of Idealism contends for the truth of some form of Realism, there is an exchange with the object of perception. But the act of sensing, feeling, perceiving, is an act of receiving, not merely the being acted upon, but the giving of hospitality to the object, opening oneself to it with all that one has, an act which is creative in a less powerful degree but in the same sense as the act of the artist. My senses are witnesses to Being, my body does not belong to me but extends into the world beyond me into which it carries me. These are some of the notions which he explores and to which he returns in order to express his sense of man as a participant in Being: our reality is a form of participation in Being. His philosophy is a study of the ways in which we do participate in Being and bear witness to Being and the ways in which we contract out and betray Being. The material world is not merely the theatre in which these themes are played out, for it is itself the Being in which we are invited to participate, and to have hate or contempt for it is blasphemy.

III

As liberty is the primary subject-object relation—the possibility in the face of life to accept or to refuse it—so fidelity is the ultimate subject-object relation. Fidelity is the attestation to Being. Therefore to re-live in reflection the experience of fidelity, unfolding its implications, is the most promising approach to the exploration of Being. I find myself engaged along with others in a world which makes demands on me: I respond to others and undertake responsibilities to and for them. So far from my being myself the ground of my certainty in knowing and the motive of my constancy in willing, it is the existence of another that gives me my primary notion of existence and it is in so far as I believe in the existence of others and act on that belief that I affirm my own existence; similarly, it is genuine response to another that initiates and can sustain the creation of my own being in fidelity. Reflection upon this core of moral experience leads to a metaphysic of Being. Whilst Marcel pursued this metaphysical inquiry in his journal, he carried on independent explorations concretely in the construction of his dramatic pieces. He says that in childhood in the domestic scene he was struck by the irreducible and irreconcilable differences manifested in the clash of temperaments and opinions. Goodwill might enter into each point of view but could not hope to reconcile them. Irreconcilable on the plane of reason and debate, there might nevertheless be an achievable harmony, as in music, beyond the irreducible objective differences. This was the constant theme of his dramatic pieces, concrete and independently pursued but cognate with his metaphysical reflections, and moving to the same issue: the affirmation of transcendence, and the refusal to abolish the stubborn contradictions of experience by recourse to abstract thinking.

Marcel seizes on Nietzsche's saying, and underlines its profundity: 'man is the only being who may make promises', bind himself and determine his future. My promise means that I dare to abstract from the illimitable world of effects and causes, which in detail I have no power to control nor even to foresee, and to treat as indifferent the changes that will occur. I dare to say that I can and will subordinate these changes to a sovereign principle. This heroic simplicity is reminiscent of antiquity (one thinks of Regulus, perhaps) but is challenged by modern ideals of sincerity, which (as Gide does, for example) insist on the value of the authenticity and spontaneity which belong to the instant and to the future and cannot be guaranteed. Hence a dilemma: when I enter into an undertaking, either I pretend to an invariability of sentiment which it is not really in my power to establish, or else I am ready to do something in the future which will not at all conform to my dispositions when I shall do it. In the first case I lie to myself, in the second I consent in advance to lie to another. Fidelity here, in the sense of constancy, self-consistency, loyalty to principle and to the past, is contrasted with sincerity, in the sense of receptivity and openness to the future. The choice is posed between the two, with the indication that the first is an impossible choice because it encloses one in a dilemma. However, both are forms of fidelity to oneself, and both are open to grave objection.

In the first case, my constancy is a point of honour, of self-esteem, which I value more highly than the content of my promise, and this if it is fidelity is a kind that makes me hateful to the person to whom I am faithful. In the second case, I make no pretence of constancy and am ready to displace myself in favour of unknown arrivals, the future states of myself. This respect for a future state of myself in which I have no permanent part is fantastic and superstitious. On this view, I have no relation to my successive states, because I have no existence save in this cinematograph run of successive states, no existence in self-recollection, no power of self-determination. The unalterability implied in the relation of fidelity is neither a pretended adherence to myself as unchangeable nor frank adherence to states of myself unalterably given. I am more than the states of myself. I am only identified with the initial state in which I take the resolution of fidelity because I fully identify myself with it in a definitive act of choice which determines my life; and I am only identified with successive states in so far as in them I am using the new circumstances to realize my promise and renew myself. What follows my promise is not a mere lapse of time in which unforeseeable changes happen to me, but a period of growth in which I realize and fulfil both my promise and myself. The inevitable changes are welcomed as occasions and inventively used as means of giving content and renewal to my promise and myself. The future is not unalterably given so that when it comes I have to accept it and identify myself with it, or else to pretend that it is other than it is; the future is not something given, a brute fact, it is to be, and what it will be is already determined in essentials, for it is my future, it is and will be me. Thus in fidelity I escape from mere becoming, passing from one discrete state of consciousness to another, because I become only what I am, what I have willed to be. This identity with myself in which I stand out of time and transcend my successive states of mind and achieve being, is no mere formal unity and no mere point of honour, for it is dynamic, it is growth, sustaining itself and becoming itself by means of the changes which it neither defies nor ignores nor accepts, but uses. And it remains continuously my will and my liberty, for I can deny myself and destroy what I proposed to be.

The concrete historical permanence which I give myself in fidelity cannot be derived from a universal law, however valid. The law is abstract and formal and governs particular cases, whereas in fidelity I continuously inform myself from within. Nor does the universal law represent or reveal more fully the objective order to which I must conform, the nature of Being, for in fidelity I am not merely cultivating an ideal, I am making a response: I am not merely being consistent with myself, but am bearing witness to an other-than-me which has hold of me. Fidelity is not a mere act of will, it is faith in the presence of an other-than-me to which I respond and to which I shall continue to respond. It is this continuous response in the bond of fidelity which is my life and my permanence, and more fully represents and reveals the structure of Being than does conformity to a law. Fidelity is response to a person and can never be rightly practised towards an idea or an ideal, which is idolatry, for a principle can make no demands upon me, because it owes the whole of its reality to the act whereby I sanction it.

The encounter between two people which leads to mutual recognition and the serious exchanges of friendship or love abolishes between them the third person which is the normal form of regard for another, and each becomes for the other a second person, a thou, and thenceforth they are together in the first person, a we. Each is present to the other and promises to be with the other always. The intimate being of each is present to the other, and fidelity is the active cultivation and enjoyment of that presence always. Absence and even death does not destroy this presence, but is rather the proof of its veritability. For when one dies whose presence I have enjoyed in friendship or in love, either he becomes less than an object or else his presence (not a mere image or memory) remains as active within me as before. It depends on my fidelity. Marcel goes so far as to say: 'To say of the dead, "they no longer exist", is not only to deny them, but to deny oneself, and perhaps to *deny* absolutely'. He means that we exist in being intimately present to each other in the fidelity of love and friendship, and to finish with this on the death of a friend is to surrender to appearances and deny the reality of the only reality. The reality of this relationship is supra-temporal, as the reality of my own being which I create by my fidelity is supra-temporal. I annihilate all being in annihilating the dead whom I have loved. This does not wholly mean keeping open the hope of immortality and reunion, but rather it means practice of the living presence of the other which remains active because it is joined to me permanently by my fidelity. The more I am present to another the more I am present to myself, the greater my density, my realization, my plenitude of being; and in the mutuality of love, belonging to one another, is an exchange of being, beyond the judgement or knowledge of a third party, which gives a concrete meaning to the notion of absolute taken strictly, and discloses a limit not of frustration but of achievement.

IV

Marcel's thought long before he became himself a professed Christian was oriented towards faith and open to revelation. He tells us how stifling and uncongenial he found the austere, moral, gloomy ethos of nineteenth-century rationalism in which he was brought up. The radiant spirit of his mother who died during his early childhood remained with him as a presence, and he sees here a profound influence upon his thinking. Before he became a believer himself, when he was thinking his way out of the Idealism which was his first love in philosophy, he was interested in the faith of others, of his friends, and in thinking himself sympathetically into an understanding of the possibility of faith he himself drew nearer to belief. Thus he can and does insist that in his strictly philosophical approaches he is still on common ground open to Christian and non-Christian. But the ground is charged with seed fallen from generations of Christian culture. And beyond Christianity there is a pagan natural piety and an orphic sense of the mystery and sacredness of life which in a world denatured by scientific handling it has become the mission of philosophy, the second movement of reflection, to recover. Brought up by an aunt who had accommodated herself by rational and moral resolves to endure living in a world which she had learned to regard as essentially uninhabitable, he had the task of finding and thinking his way back into a world in which he could breathe and love and hope. The world which he restores is a world which is indeed incomplete and in mortal danger, and for that reason cries out for and recognizes Christian salvation, but it is a world which can be saved, which goes half way to meet its salvation. Man is bound to his life in the world by a nuptial tie which he can undo, but in so far as he does cut himself loose he loses the sense of his personal existence.

In any case, Marcel, although the obedient churchman, is never the orthodox theologian. His theology is always a highly personal reflection upon experience. In a characteristic metaphor, translated from his musical interests, existence is *l'Improvisation absolu* in which I participate more and more effectively, more and more intelligently, a conception which has broken with all Idealism and marks, as he notes, the transition from the Bergsonian philosophy of creative evolution to a religious philosophy. Even as philosopher, as reflective mind looking on at what is going on, I am not mere spectator but continue to participate with a change of role. This metaphor of the improvisation changes places with the metaphor of the lost Atlantis, the submerged continent of Being which is all lying there and crops out above the surface. Whatever the metaphors used, there is a persistent sense of Being as enfolding my own being and the other beings who are present to me and to whom I am present, like a mother liquid in which it is my true destiny to remain in solution and my perpetual tendency to crystallize out.

Beyond participation is permeability, if I open myself, bring myself to the point of holding myself as permeable: it is for me to consent or to refuse; or to pass from refusal to consent, to invocation. We are waited for and watched at every moment by despair and betrayal, and death is there at the end of our visible career with a standing invitation to the absolute defection. The essence of our world is perhaps betrayal. But that possibility, always to be reckoned with, is not a final reason for ourselves assuming it. If I decide to live in faith, hope, and charity, cultivating patience and humility in profound dependence upon God, I am playing for a stake which I believe to exist and to be worth the loss of everything else: I am affirming what I am over against what I have, and my life is the venture I make. To do this would be more than risky, it would be culpable, if I were not making a response to what comes home to me as an appeal. My only excuse for flying in the face of appearances and breaking with rational conclusions is that I have made myself open, have been ready to hear, and have been called. I respond, I enter into the engagement of faith, I take up a transcendental point of view from which the conditions and facts of ordinary human experience look out of place and inexplicable. My assurance is inward and cannot be translated into objective proofs, my justification is not a process of impersonal investigation but my own witness invited and supported by the attestation of others; for my relation to God, like my relation to my friend, is not in the third person: God is not he but thou, the absolute Thou. The absolute Thou cannot be thought; the believer is wholly present in his own invocation and strives to live in the presence of this wholly Other in a unique relationship which cannot be communicated. The unbeliever can learn to recognize the necessarily personal nature of this faith from his own experience of communication in its ideal transcendence, and (like Marcel himself) can begin by believing in the faith of others, until this openness to belief leads to his own call and his own response. The believer is the witness to the existence and power of his God, and proves his testimony by the Christian quality of the personality which his fidelity creates. This is the testimony, the fidelity of the Church, deriving from the original witness of the Apostles. Christianity begins with the recognition of Christ on the road to Emmaus (which Marcel puts in juxtaposition with the recognition of Ulysses by Eumaeos), that is to say, with recognition of the historical permanence, the existential reality, to which fidelity bears witness, the living presence of another which fidelity creates and absence and death cannot destroy. In such a case, to bear witness is also to call to witness, that is, to appeal to another for confirmation, to declare whether or not my witness is true by bearing witness himself.

This privileged knowledge which I have of a person whom I speak to as thou, how does it differ from common impersonal knowledge? If it has access to Being, denied to objective knowledge, what kind of knowledge is it and how is it known not to be illusory? In treating another as an object open to public inquiry I can build up a precise and objective knowledge of him in which he is one like myself and all others. In my communion with him as thou I do not add to this kind of knowledge of him, what I know is not his common human nature but his personal existence, his presence in what he gives himself to and his presence with me. It is this exercise of his liberty which makes him not merely another but himself, a personal existence and not merely a human being. It is his presence or absence, his power to give or to withhold himself, that I experience, and this is his personal being which cannot be known objectively. In so far as I am open to him, present with him (that is, treat him as thou), I help him to be free, to give himself and to be present. In so far as I am truly open to him, it is he that is present with me, not my idea of him. And in so far as I have my idea or my ideal of him I am not truly open to him and do not experience him as present.

Thus the engagement of fidelity is beset with risks: not only may I be deceived in the object of my faith, who may abuse my confidence, but also I may be deceiving myself with an idea or an ideal of him. It is these risks which are eliminated in the engagement of faith. It is not initiated by mutual attraction, for indeed the appearances of the world invite the contrary. Since God cannot deceive me and I have no justification for having any ideas or ideals of him, there can be no question of a change in the subject or object which could justify a denial. It is not one engagement amongst others, it is the foundation of all, since God alone has access to the interior of any and is the ultimate bond of all. It is the absolute engagement, which I cannot deny without a total denial of myself, with the totality of Being.

V

The theory of the second person (the thou), the presence of two persons to each other, their being with each other and belonging to each other, cultivating in fidelity the we which thou and I create, implies the notion of disposability (*disponibilité*), the readiness to bestow and spend oneself and make oneself available, and its contrary, indisposability. 'When I am with someone who is indisposable, I am conscious of being with someone for whom I do not exist; I am then thrown back on myself.' To be indisposable is to be self-absorbed, that is, to be fixed in the realm of having and to be restless, gloomy, and anxious by condition, to be possessed by a vague unquiet which in relation to particular objects on which interest fixes hardens into despair, for I tend to identify myself with what I have and to reflect that when I no longer have anything I shall no longer be anything. But I exist in the first place because I can dispose of what I have, sacrifice it, even sacrifice my life—and the martyr's existence is the testimony created by his sacrifice. It is by means of my body that I dispose of what I have, but I cannot dispose of my body, I leave it to others to dispose of. That is the image and the fate of my indisposability. When I dispose of myself, because I am it is a living presence I leave behind: I am more than what I have, because others have been present to me, real and valued.

I am present not only to others whom I love but also in my acts when they are truly mine. An act is certified by being owned, owned to. To face, to challenge, to take responsibility for, to take upon oneself, to evaluate, these are the acts characteristic of personal existence, and they are acts in which the person is fully present. They are the kind of act in which the person not only comes to himself but in which at the same time he intervenes in the impersonal world of third parties to whom we are all the time equivocally related, the impersonal 'one' in oneself and in the other on which everyday life is built and which stands to personal existence much as having stands to being. In such acts I am not only fully present, I go beyond myself, I respond; there is the combination of initiative and receptivity characteristic of creativity in all its forms: I am *disponible*, hospitable.

It may be said: 'I tend to make myself indisposable precisely in so far as I treat my life or my being as something I have which is in some sense a quantity liable to dilapidation, exhaustion, or even evaporation'. That is the source of chronic anxiety and care which dries up the soul and checks every generous initiative. Despair, despair of the universe, pessimism has the same roots as indisposability; and the more one is indisposable the less use he has for hope. Living in the world of having, he desires and fears, but cannot hope, for he has no faith. On the other hand, the soul exists only by hope, it breathes hope. To hope is not to refuse to fear, but to refuse to despair of the universe, to give it credit, to believe in its order, its integrity, the ultimate security of values. Philosophically, this is the work of reflection, but it only succeeds if it leads to ventures, to disposability and participation, and to permeability and the supreme venture of faith at the limit, an absolute engagement contracted by the totality of myself and addressed to the totality of Being. If I despair, it is my own choice. If I am disposable, fidelity is only the chief of many experiences by which I participate in the inexhaustibility of Being and taste its power to satisfy. The tourist runs restlessly round and ticks off the sights indicated in his guide-book; it is a famous place and abounds in interesting things, but they are soon exhausted and boredom is round the corner. At home in his own country the life in which he participates is not reducible to a catalogue of items, a desert of objects, and is not exhaustible. It is the difference between having and being. Nevertheless, the very experience of inexhaustible value in the world is an insufficiency which becomes an invocation, since it is threatened on all sides.

Is hope efficacious? It is not a technique, a magic to have recourse to when practical techniques fail. Nor is it an excuse for laziness, leaving to God what we should do ourselves. It is only in place when we are invited to despair because our personal helplessness is indeed absolute and there is nothing to be done. Then it is the completion of our activity, not a substitute for it; it is the river of our own striving which flows on out of sight and empties itself in an invisible sea, a refusal to calculate the possibilities and be limited by the result of our calculation, a leap over the visible calculable ground, a prophecy. The possibility of hope coincides strictly with that of despair. Death is the springboard of an absolute hope, as it is the invitation to an absolute despair. Hope is the province, the prerogative, the life of the soul; it is to desire what patience is to passivity; it is an act of will sustained by faith: it says, prophetically, This shall be—as the lover says to his love, You shall not die.

Being is incalculable because inexhaustible, and that is the ground of joy and hope. If its contents could be listed in an inventory and its transactions accounted for by strict book-keeping, there could be no source of joy and no room for hope. But for Marcel, the incalculable on which hope relies is the supernatural: 'Hope is only possible in a world in which there is a place for miracles'. The model of all hope is the hope of salvation, which means for the Christian the hope of attaining contemplation, living in the presence of God. But salvation has no meaning unless things have really gone wrong; faith in the integrity of the universe, on which hope is grounded, only means something in a world which is rent by real and serious breaks. Otherwise, if there are no real gaps and wounds, if the world can be shown to be rational and coherent, there is no need of salvation but only of wisdom, no need of hope but only of personal elevation, no need of Christianity but only of stoicism or Spinozism. It is from the bottom of my need that I launch my appeal to the highest point of transcendence: 'I believe in thee who art my sole recourse'.

VI

The main jet of Marcel's thinking, like all existentialism, is forced from the conclusion that the type of thought which dominates or encloses or sees through its object is necessarily inapplicable to the total situation in which the thinker himself as existing individual is enclosed, and therefore every system (since in principle a system of thought is outside the thinker and transparent to him) is a mere invention and the most misleading of false analogies. The thinker is concerned with the interior of the situation in which he is enclosed: with his own internal reality, rather than with the collection of qualities by which he is defined or the external relations by which his position is plotted; and with his own participation in the situation, rather than with the inaccessible view of its externality. His thought refers to a self which can only be pre-supposed and not thought and to a situation in which he is involved and which he therefore cannot fully envisage; so that in the nature of the case philosophic thought cannot have the complete clarity and mastery of scientific thought which deals with an object in general for a subject in general. To look for this type of thinking in philosophy is to overlook the necessary conditions of human thinking on ultimate questions; for philosophers to produce it at this time of day is sheer paralysis induced by superstitious regard for the prestige of contemporary science or of the classical philosophies. Philosophy, as Jaspers said, can nerve the thinker by reflection upon the conditions of thinking to dare to think that there is a reality which cannot be thought. In that case, Being can be experienced, indicated, attested, but not represented and possessed.

This reality which is beyond the subject-object relation of scientific thought is not, to begin with, the object of religious faith. In the first place, it can be located and precisely indicated to reflection in the experience of the thinker. My existence in liberty, disposing of what I have, saying yes or no to my life, by its very nature is open to doubt and denial in theory and in practice; it is not problematic, to be disposed of one way or the other by means of an empirical investigation; it is a metaphysical reality, inaccessible, presupposed, a mystery. Although it is my absolute reality, the source and secret of all that has value in my life, it can be ignored, denied, or betrayed. This transcendental I cannot exist unless the transcendental thou also exists; they can be with each other and present to each other, and help to maintain each other's transcendence, spiritual reality, and activity. This fidelity, only possible at the level of transcendence, and maintained by vital activity and continual presence, is the highest level of human life, the essential human life, and the philosophical clue to Being. To relapse altogether into objective modes and standards of thought and behaviour (from this level of self-possession and self-disposal maintained by and maintaining the self-possession and self-disposal of others) is a degradation. Personal existence is an experienced reality which can be clarified and confirmed by reflection and indicated to others: it can be tested and attested.

The experience of personal existence, with its incarnation and its transcendence, suggests a transcendental I AM WHAT I AM standing to the created universe not precisely as I stand to my body and my life, but similarly: an absolute I who is to each believer an absolute Thou. Each believer is a witness, and the non-believer begins by belief in the other's belief. The Church meets the plausibility of the suggestion with the confirmation of its historical reaffirmed attestation.

The metaphysical experience and the religious faith are separable, and the first although it suggests does not necessarily imply the other. A divine order in the world cannot be inferred from nature nor from history and the rational proofs of the existence of God have no efficacy with one who is not disposed to believe; appearances are strongly against belief. On the other hand are the experiences which powerfully promote hope and faith. The world is ambiguous and incalculable. In any case we have to live, and cannot postpone so vital a decision indefinitely whilst we balance probabilities which can never conclude the business for us. We are not disinterested, we are infinitely interested. If we are infinitely interested in believing or (for whatever reason) in disbelieving, that is the main matter—as Kierkegaard perceived. The probabilities are irrelevant because they can never take into account the real evidence, for it is only by recovering our positive immediacy through reflective qualification of our rational modes of thought that we become capable of the tender response, the blind intuition, which is the foetal form of faith; once released, that primal responsiveness gains strength from reason and experience, makes itself disposable and permeable, and invokes the call to which faith is the mature response.

Marcel makes the position of the unbeliever look much less intellectually and morally respectable than it is usually held to be. He removes the issue to a universe of discourse in which Butler's conclusion does not hold, that 'to *us*, probability is the very guide of life'. We are not asked to make up our minds whether or not something that we cannot see is really there; we are shown that the only reasonable thing to do is to retrace our steps to another point of view, and look. This is the great strength and the great weakness of Marcel: his strength because he really does restore a dimension of reason which logical thinking lacks; his weakness because he has too little use for the help of our insignificant four-cornered human reason. He is a miniaturist who has chosen to work in the third dimension only, and the results are baffling. But where there is great strength, it is not weakness that has the last word.

V

MARTIN HEIDEGGER

(Born 1889)

Catholic

I

HEIDEGGER's main systematic work, *Sein und Zeit* (1927), made an impression and roused expectations, for it disclosed not only his originality and professional accomplishment but also the ambitious scope of his thought, which, reckoning with Kant and avoiding the illusory standpoint of Hegel, aimed at building a metaphysic of Being on the scale of Plato and Aristotle, and which showed that it had already assimilated and brought into its focus the thought of the most original thinkers of the age, such as Kierkegaard, Nietzsche, Bergson, Dilthey, Husserl, Scheler, and Simmel. The plan of his work has not yet been carried out, and it is perhaps unlikely now that it will be. Critics have confidently said that his first volume digs away the ground on which he proposes to build his metaphysic of Being, and for that reason the work is not likely to be proceeded with. Nevertheless, the fragments of later work which have been published show plainly enough what the present trend of his thought is and that it is consistent with his original aim: it may be said that the programme is being carried out, although not systematically in treatment. Heidegger insistently dissociates himself from existential philosophy, for, he says, he is concerned with the problem of Being, not with personal existence and its ethical interests, the human condition as such. For all that, he is inescapably put amongst the existentialists because he is one of them in his themes and ideas and in his treatment of them and in the language he uses, as well as in his debt to Kierkegaard and in his influence upon the others, especially upon Sartre.

Heidegger's philosophy, then, proposes to raise the question, What is Being, what is what is? His method derives from Husserl to whose chair at Freiburg he succeeded in 1929. Husserl's standpoint in philosophy was not existentialist, but his influence upon existentialist philosophers is incalculable, and it is safe to say that existentialism in its modern phase would not have developed without him. Kierkegaard has profoundly influenced Protestant theology, and has influenced Jaspers and Heidegger, but it is as one of the developments of Husserl's fruitful school of pure phenomenology that existentialism takes its place in contemporary technical philosophy. Husserl himself was a mathematician and logician, philosophically interested in the world of experience rather than in the experienced world. His method proposed to put the real world within brackets and disconnect the consciousness of it, switching attention inwards instead to the absolute world of experience itself, exploring and describing the structure of consciousness in its intuiting of essences, dispensing of meanings, and constitution of objects. His ambition was of the greatest, nothing less than to found philosophy for the first time on its proper basis in pure phenomenological description, uncovering in all their ramifications the root structures of all possible knowledge, 'as it were, the secret longing of the whole philosophy of modern times', a science towards which the fundamental thought of Descartes was already pressing, whose domain Hume almost entered, which Kant caught sight of but was not able to appropriate; a science of all sciences, not in order to appropriate and systematize their results, but, on the contrary, in order to constitute their beginnings, map their regional structures, and fix their defining essences. Such a science, with its unlimited programme of research, could only be inspired by the most radical rationalism, philosophically determined to force a way back to an absolute beginning, to accept nothing as given or problematic, and to get such a command of the essentially necessary structures of experience that the real world might be seen as a special case of various possible worlds and non-worlds all experiencable in principle. Such a project may be a mathematician's dream, but it has many features of exceptional interest and has already proved itself as a remarkably stimulating and fruitful initiative. Husserl boldly refused to relinquish the ancient ambition of philosophy to render Being fully intelligible, and as boldly he proscribed past and present errors and set his hand to a prodigious co-operative task that promised to do it. The existentialists, without his mathematician's bias, use his method of discerning and describing basic structures, but with their attention turned back to the world, including the self in the world. And when we return to the factual world, we find that we can constitute, and therefore explain, meanings, but we cannot constitute, and therefore cannot explain, the real; we are up against an irreducible existence which we must accept and can describe but cannot constitute, although we can constitute its meanings. Existence is an inexhaustible reservoir of meanings, since our approach to things is always and necessarily from a point of view and is therefore drastically selective. But Heidegger wishes to raise the question of the meaning of Being in its unity and totality.

He begins from the natural point of view, arguing that since we are not outside Being and able to stand in relation to it as we do to an object of thought, we shall have to proceed indirectly by examining particular types of existents. Human existence is obviously indicated as the starting point, since we are privileged in our relation to that, and since any metaphysic of Being must itself be a product of this human existent. The first task is to uncover the structure of human existence.

Dasein (the word, although ambiguously used by Heidegger, is generally accepted as an untranslatable technical term of his philosophy, meaning the mode of existence of the human being) is not to be conceived on the analogy of a thing as a substance with properties. 'The essence of *Dasein* is in its existence.' This simply means that human reality cannot be defined because it is not something given, it is in question. A man is possibility, he has the power to be. His existence is in his choice of the possibilities which are open to him, and since this choice is never final, once for all, his existence is indeterminate because not terminated. Nevertheless, the mode of existence of the human being has a structure: it is being-in-the-world. This being-in-the-world which constitutes human being is the being of a self in its inseparable relations with a not-self, the world of things and other persons in which the self always and necessarily finds itself inserted. This manner of existence is not merely accidental, it is a necessity of thought in the sense that the world as I find it is constitutive of my existence, not merely the place in which I have my existence. There is no separation possible. My preoccupations in the world, my tasks, concerns, cares, pursuits, exemplify the manner of my existence: I can free myself from this or that task or care, but never from preoccupation of some sort. My immediate world (the world immediately present to me) is the world of my preoccupations, my concerns, not the world of objects immediately present. Similarly, the objects with which I am concerned are not so much things as tools, that is, things of specific use to me and systematically bound to other things in the service of my interests. The tool, related to other tools in an elaborate system of regular, serviceable, but modifiable relations, is the typical thing or object in the world; and this type of existent is described by Heidegger as being-ready-to-hand (*Zuhandenheit*). This is the primitive meaning of objects or things, and remains their fundamental concrete meaning; like *Dasein* they are constituted by their relations to other things in the world and to an existent of the nature of *Dasein*: the needle implies the thread, the garment, the sewer, and the wearer. That is to say, the object as tool is constituted by the system of relations in which it exists, and refers to and ends in *Dasein*, which is itself constituted by its relations to the system but refers to its own possibilities and not to the system for its meaning. *Dasein* as possibility (the source of possibilities) and constituted by relations with objects as tools in a serviceable system (enabling possibilities to be realized) gives intelligibility to the world as the realization of projects.

This view of the world is in strong contrast to the abstract rationalist view derived from Descartes, in which the rational is the real, and mathematical physics the classical type of knowledge—and the laws of nature ultimately more important than nature. The contrast of the concrete approach by way of our preoccupations as inserted in the world and all the time actively engaged with it is exemplified in the different conceptions of space. The abstract geometric space of mathematical physics contrasts with the qualitative space of actual preoccupations which is inseparable from the objects: the place where the object is determines its nature and conditions its function; the brake is not a brake unless it is on the wheel, and its being in place in turn creates the stable conditions of the environment. A place for everything, and everything in its place, is the conception of space in our daily preoccupations—and 'there is a time for everything' shows a conception of time rooted in our concerns. The conception of classical physics (in modern physics all spatial propositions refer solely to the behaviour of bodies, never to 'space') has led to the popular conception of one thing amongst others in a space. This is a false conception of the world of objects, still more of *Dasein*. Their relations, spatial and other, are constitutive of *Dasein* and the things in the world. *Dasein* has the inherent tendency to annihilate space, to extend the senses and enlarge the world, and to determine and organize the world, physically and psychologically, in terms of preoccupation. Man employs and modifies, extends and improves his tools in the pursuit of his projects, and thus actively uses time for the realization of his possibilities. It is in this way that he constitutes an intelligible world.

This contrast between the meaning we give the world in the practical ordering of our daily affairs and the rational construction of a world of objects in space and time is not a contrast between practice and theory, preoccupation and science, but between a correct appreciation of the intelligible structure of the world revealed in a descriptive analysis of practice and popular misconceptions derived from the unrecognized abstractions of an obsolete science and philosophy. There is no conflict between a practical interpretation of the world and a scientific interpretation: both are co-ordinate perspectives. To say that the hammer is heavy may mean that it is unwieldy or that it has a weight, can be weighed. The hammer can be regarded as a tool (*Zuhandene*) or as a given object (*Vorhandene*), as something ready-to-hand or merely as something at-hand, present. Science deals with objects from a limited point of view determined in advance, limits its interest to certain phenomena and on that basis settles its methods and its criteria. To regard the hammer as a body having weight is a restricted view for a special purpose. Science is not privileged but specialized, not *the* interpretation of the world but a selected aspect, not an experience in use of the concrete object handled in the perspective of man's projects but a break-down into abstractions taken out of the system of concrete relations and assimilated to another system of meanings determined by special questions raised within the perspective of the project of Nature.

My being-in-the-world, in this sense of being constituted by my projects and by my relations with the objects which I make use of and develop as tools for realizing them, involves my being-with-others who are also in the world in the same sense. Here again, the existence of others is not merely accidental, nor a problem for thought, but is a necessity of thought, is constitutive of my being and implied in it, as the barber as barber implies the customer, and the needle as needle both the thread and the cloth, and the seamstress and the wearer. The nature of *Dasein* is being-in-common, human existence is a shared existence and the social interdependence of our everyday experience is primordial and constitutive. My full self-consciousness and self-affirmation derive from my consciousness of others: it is not that I begin with myself as given and indubitable and somehow deduce the existence of others like myself. Thus I am constituted both by my preoccupations in which I make use of objects as tools and by my solicitude for persons.

Just as one can free oneself from this or that preoccupation but not from preoccupation of some sort, so one can free oneself from dependence upon this or that person but not from social relations altogether. Indeed, escape from servitude to other persons may deliver one more completely into the hands of the ubiquitous dictator of everyday human affairs, the impersonal one, *das Man*. Heidegger, like Kierkegaard in his account of the Public, describes the process by which each one in a necessary conformity to established usages, judgements, and opinions, is assimilated to the general forms of human existence. This is the great alibi, the proof that all the time I was in respectable company, the flight from personal responsibility, the escape into anonymity. Always there is the prescription of what *one* should do in such a case, and the frown on what is not done. Assimilation to this established general form of human existence necessarily means the sacrifice of my own possibilities, the I remains buried in the one. But I gain the solidity and assurance of this massive existence, and I reinforce it with my own acquiescence. To resist and break with this mode of existence in order to realize other possibilities would create a crisis in my personal life. There is in me the strongest tendency to avoid the issue, to take refuge from my original situation, the human plight, in the comfort and assurance of this anonymous and approved mode of existence. And that is what leads me to misinterpret my situation, virtually to think of myself as a thing in a world of things, as a given substance with given properties, and thus to take refuge from myself as existing solely in my relations and my acts, as possibility, as having to choose and project myself. But in any case, the impersonal structure of social life also is constitutive of the mode of existence of the human being, because *Dasein* is being-in-common. *Dasein* cannot get rid of this impersonal mode of being: I can only modify it. But that makes all the difference. To be 'one like many' is ambiguous and, as Kierkegaard had put it, 'to will to live as a particular human being . . . in the same sense as is open to every other human being, is the ethical victory over life and all its illusions'.

First, however, what is this original human situation obscured by everyday existence and which we are impelled to hide from ourselves? I am in-the-world in the sense described; it is an existence not chosen but having to be chosen, not asked for but demanding to be taken charge of, disclosing itself to me as a simple fact of which I have to bear the burden without knowing why or whence or whither. My primordial sense of this situation is the root of my affective life; all my emotions and sentiments derive from it and obscurely refer to it. From this sense of my finitude (*Befindlichkeit*) also derives my whole interpretation of the world and my capacity to respond to it, for it is a sense not merely of limitation but also of possibility and of imperative: I am and I must be. Otherwise, a world in which we were not merely finite but also finished, a world in which we were not implicated, by which we were not constituted, in which we had no part to play, could not exist for us; if, *per impossibile*, we could look at it as pure spectators, we should be indifferent, that is to say, we could not see it. As it is, my dereliction in the world, and my sense of this solitude and abandonment, the fundamental motive and situation of my whole life, can never be fully overcome because my achievement of myself can never be final, never ceases to require my projects and therefore my interest in the world, and therefore it is this dereliction which constitutes my existence for myself and my power to comprehend and interpret the world.

Dasein, then, being possibility, exists by projecting itself, and these tentative projects (*Entwurf*) are interpretations, not conceptual but existential. My comprehension of the world (*Verstehen*) springs together with my sense of being cast into the world (*Befindlichkeit*) from a common root in the basic human situation, for I recognize what I exist for in my possibilities and what the things about me exist for in their answering to my possibilities. The meaning of human existence is elaborated in the possibilities of action of *Dasein*. I give sense to what is about me by making use of it. But this construction (rather than perception) is limited by the nature of things: not everything is possible, it is not a dream world, but a world of brute existence already elaborated and organized into routine possibilities by the realizations of others. This opens to me two decisively opposed modes of being: authentic being rooted in the explicit sense of my situation (*Befindlichkeit*); and inauthentic being, moving automatically in the established ruts and routes of the organized world.

These existential interpretations of human existence (*Entwurf*), realized possibilities, are not in themselves intellectual conceptions, they are forms of human being; but all forms of knowledge derive from them. Any of the possible human activities, shoeing a horse for example, may be carried on without explicit consciousness of what is being done, and usually is; but the agent may stand back from his operation and look at it critically or analytically, thinking the hammer as hammer and the anvil as anvil. Even to take a lighter hammer is implicitly to conceive of the hammer as hammer. The meaning of any object is thought in relation to proposed or possible activities of *Dasein* in realizing projects. Logical judgements are founded ultimately on existential interpretations which are not conceptual at all.

Dasein, moved by this obscure sense of its existence as possibility, and realizing itself tentatively in existential interpretations, must have the power of articulating and discriminating alternatives based on a recognition of the use of things (*Verstehen*), and this is the existential root of language (*Rede*). Language implies communication and embodies the existence-in-common which is *Dasein*. Thus language also is constitutive of *Dasein*.

Since *Dasein* gives meaning to brute existence in terms of its projects, it creates truth: it finds a place and a use in its intelligible world for what is in chaos, and thus uncovers what is there, allows the existent to manifest itself, to come into the world, to show what it is. *Dasein* by its nature is *lumen naturale*, for its existence is to stand out from the world and to become something in the world, and in so doing it throws light on what is there, and indeed makes it that there is a world. This creation of the truth is not subjective nor arbitrary because it proceeds from the nature of *Dasein* whose structure is universal, and because it is projected on and limited by the independently real: it is the meaning of existence which is created and not existence itself.

Language communicates truth, that is, uncovers and calls attention to what is there. But everyday language in constant use loses touch with the objects to which it ostensibly refers; as Bacon says, words are substituted for things. Language then spreads untruth and establishes inauthentic existence. Instead of mediating my being-in-the-world by revealing intelligible objects of use and enjoyment, it obscures them by covering them with itself; the intermediary becomes the principal and the true principal is displaced. Everyday language which spreads untruth becomes more authoritative than the truth because the reference by which it should be authenticated is obscured and forgotten and therefore raises no question; what commonly 'is said' passes because there is nobody there to be challenged. Losing touch with real existents, we turn from one thing to another, seeking accomplishments, insatiable in curiosity, living a 'full', 'intellectual', 'interesting' life, becoming alienated, uprooted, severed from oneself, others, and the world. In this way one remains, or insensibly comes to be, without a sense of the original situation which is the abiding root of one's whole emotional, cognitive, and active life; the existential interpretations which realize the possibilities of *Dasein* are simply and without clear choice taken over from the impersonal modes of existence elaborated in the everyday world, a world of echoed and distorted meanings substituting itself for the genuinely intelligible world of authentic existence.

Hiding from oneself in the many forms of impersonal existence is inspired by 'dread'. Kierkegaard had analysed 'the concept of dread' in order to penetrate to the deepest layer of human feeling, and Heidegger uses it for the same purpose. Dread differs from fear in seeming to have no object and no cause, and that is what makes it so profoundly disturbing, and at the same time that makes it easier to smother, so that it is seldom felt in its intensity and clarity; one assigns some cause and passes it off, for its meaning is that we are unwilling to face what it indicates, and turn instead to the solid assurances of common sense upheld by the authority of the impersonal dictator of everyday life. But although it can be avoided it is too authentic to be extirpated, and it can be analysed. The decisive character of dread is that it cannot be localized and it refuses to be pinned down to anything in which we are interested and which we feel to be threatened, by emptying everything in the world of all interest for me; it invests everything alike with a common worthlessness. When I see that it is nothing in the world that inspires this dread I see that it is the world itself as such: what inspires my dread is my recognition of what it means to-be-in-the-world, when I see this in its totality and not merely in the perspectives of my particular preoccupations. Dread withdraws me from my preoccupations, encloses me in a solitude, where I am forced to choose whether I will be myself or not. In this moment my personal reality is revealed to me and henceforward I have chosen what I will to be. For dread separates me from the interests and meanings of my life in the world, absorbed and lost in my relations and preoccupations, and isolates me in this recognition that I can either continue this impersonally determined inauthentic existence or by heroic effort take personal charge of my own existence, and that in any case I never am but always will be, because I can will to be. Thus dread which at first in contrast to fear is so vague and meaningless proves the most specific and significant of all emotions, a pitiless pointing to my original situation, an awful anticipation of my personal choice, a fear of being already cast into the world and a fear for my authenticity in living in the world.

It is dread, then, that reveals *Dasein*, the mode of existence of the human being, to oneself and founds *Befindlichkeit*, the sense of the situation and vital attitude in face of it. *Dasein* is seen to be an existence already found in the world in the condition of becoming, and therefore facing an open future with the power to be, and bound up with other beings encountered in the world. This structure of *Dasein* is named by Heidegger Care (*Sorge*), and it is important to be clear about the three elements which constitute it. Personal existence is self-projecting, it is not what it is but what it will be, because it is not formed and finished but has an open future; therefore structurally it is in advance of itself, there is something to come, and its concern for what it is to be is expressed in the term *Care*. But Care also includes my being already found in a world in which this personal existence has to be realized. Finally, Care expresses my being in the grip of particular relations and preoccupations in this world. Care, then, is the structure of the mode of existence of one who exists by anticipating what he will be in a world in which he is found and to which he is bound.

What is meant by describing as anticipation the self-projection of personal existence into the future has now to be explained. Personal existence, being always what it will be, never simply and solely what it is, has no finality and totality of its own and is never achieved. When death supervenes its possibilities are extinguished but not exhausted. Moreover, death does not strike me down, it is not an accident which happens to me, it is from the very beginning one of my own possibilities which I nurse within me. Indeed, it *is* my possibility eminently, because its realization is inevitable and will be realized by me in the most authentically personal way without any possibility of avoidance or substitution. Further, it is a possibility which not only has empire over all other possibilities, since it eventually extinguishes them, but which also has a bearing upon them whilst they remain options; for it reveals their contingency: if I can die, I need not have existed, nobody need exist, personal existence is launched between nothingness and nothingness and it is nothingness that is real, everything is absurd, the impossibility of existence is possible, nothing is necessary. Thus my death is for me the capital possibility, always in view from the outset, from which all other possibilities derive their status of radical contingency. What dread reveals to me is that I am cast into the world in order to die there. This is the truth of our situation which is hidden from us by our daily preoccupations and by the authority of the impersonal mode of social existence upheld by common sense. Personal existence, then, which is possibility and therefore cannot be characterized as a whole or seized as given, can be seized by the definitive nature of its capital possibility: if I am always what I will be, at least it is always certain what I will be.

Death, then, is the clue to authentic living, the eventual and omnipresent possibility which binds together and stabilizes my existence. I am projected in advance of myself becoming what I will be, whether I will to be or not, but I can anticipate here and now what I will be, not waiting for the end, and this is the only way in which I can command and possess my existence and give it unity and authenticity. I anticipate death not by suicide but by living in the presence of death as always immediately possible and as undermining everything. This full-blooded acceptance (*amor fati*) of death, lived out, is authentic personal existence. Everything is taken as contingent. Everything is devalued. Personal existence and everything encountered in personal existence is accepted as nothing, as meaningless, fallen under the blow of its possible impossibility. I see all my possibilities as already annihilated in death, as they will be, like those of others in their turn. In face of this capital possibility which devours all the others, there are only two alternatives: acceptance or distraction. Even this choice is a rare privilege, since few are awakened by dread to the recognition of the choice, most remain lost in the illusions of everyday life. To choose acceptance of death as the supreme and normative possibility of my existence is not to reject the world and refuse participation in its daily preoccupations, it is to refuse to be deceived and to refuse to be identified with the preoccupations in which I engage: it is to take them for what they are worth—

nothing. From this detachment springs the power, the dignity, the tolerance of authentic personal existence.

If I am awakened from the illusions of everyday life and brought to confront the choice which is open to me, it is by the voice of conscience. The voice of conscience which seems to be telling us what to do and what not to do is really in this form what it is often held to be, the voice of *das Man*, the impersonal ruler, the powers that be, father, god. But conscience is there in the structure of my existence as possibility, in the fact that whatever I am doing I can identify myself with it or not, and that at bottom I can take charge of my whole existence or not. Conscience is witness to this alternative of authenticity or inauthenticity. It accuses me of living inauthentic-ally, not of doing this wrong or the other, for authenticity consists in the manner of living, not in what is done. And when it calls me to live authentically it also invites me to recognize and live in the know-ledge of my irremediable culpability which cannot be atoned for nor remedied like a particular guilt. The conscience that calls, accuses, and judges is already within the structure of Care, that is, the *Dasein* as possibility and as already thrown into the world and bound up with everyday existence: it is *Dasein* as possibility calling *Dasein* embodied and dispersed in the impersonal 'one' of everyday life. The culpability which I fasten on myself is not the guilt of living inauthentically but the guilt of resolving to live authentically; it is original, for the *Dasein*, whatever it does, is itself the source of evil so soon as it assumes and accepts an existence of which it can never be master; it is culpable whatever it does so soon as it accepts and takes responsibility for a finite existence irretrievably determined and doomed. All particular faults and wrongs are metaphysically founded in this culpable nature of *Dasein*. When I accept with fully open eyes my existence as I find it to be, issuing from nothing into nothing, and I live it out in the light of that understanding, I make myself culpable. The alternative is to remain inauthentic, not to rise to the specifically human quality of living, or to reject personal existence with the definitiveness of suicide or of Eastern nihilism. If this account of conscience seems very strange, and at variance with the deliverances of the moral consciousness, the answer is that the moral conscious-ness is saturated with the demands of inauthentic everyday existence and requires to be sifted and clarified before it is a true guide: more-over, the last thing we want to do is to go in the direction in which it would offer to take us. Again, in this notion of culpability as the acceptance of full responsibility for our finite personal existence Heidegger, like Jaspers, follows Kierkegaard.

Authentic personal existence, then, responding to the call of conscience, is clear-sighted and resolved, consents to exist for death, actively identifies itself with its own nothingness without hope of overcoming it, and for that reason recognizes and accepts its guilt. In using these terms Heidegger disavows any ethical intention, and insists throughout that he is solely interested in the structure of *Dasein*, the mode of existence of the human being, as a necessary preliminary to the understanding of Being in its totality. Authentic personal existence is personal existence which is resolved, which has faced its sovereign possibility and taken its decision to live perpetually in anticipation of it; apart from any moral achievement which this may be, it constitutes personal existence in its totality which can therefore be known, and when personal existence understands itself it also understands the world: that is Heidegger's professed theme.

In any case, Heidegger points out, a philosophy cannot pretend and does not attempt to prescribe to the individual what he shall do (least of all an existential philosophy, which insists on the uniqueness of the concrete individual). It gives the general determination of human being, the master perspective which commands all possibilities: the concrete decisions, the actual possibilities of each personal existence to be realized in daily life, are left to the make-up and history of the person and to his liberty and the circumstances of the case. A philosophy which does otherwise loses both its universality and its concreteness and becomes abstract, for its prescriptions violate both the personal will and the individuality of the case, whereas a philosophy which restricts itself to general orientation puts the individual in the way of seeing what is there and throws the particular facts of the case into relief against the background of the general situation, and thus combines universality with concreteness in a way that is fertilizing and decisive. Thus orientation does in practice go a long way towards the determination of individual decisions. Authentic personal existence resolves not only to live steadily in the light of its sovereign possibility which devalues everything but also to accept what has been determined by the actualities of individual inheritance and past actions and what is determined by the social actualities which sustain everyday life in the world, as a trader accepts the terms of trade. Authentic personal existence is a synthesis of the imposed and the willed, and the synthesis is achieved by taking up the imposed into the willed: I will my own past and the world as it is given in the immediate circumstances and in its ultimate interpretation, and with my will self-determined in this way I choose from the possibilities which remain open. This requires a constant effort on my part, it is a conquest always insecure, never a victory outright. Consistent orientation towards death, which breaks the pretensions of everything which claims attention, my own pretensions above all, without any slackening of responsibility and energy in choosing and fulfilling the possibilities that are open on each occasion, that alone is the mode of existence of the enlightened and resolved human being. But the resolution is an individual resolution informing a unique personal existence, not a general philosophic inference from a descriptive analysis of the mode of existence of the human being, and the function of the notions of conscience, guilt, and resolve in Heidegger's analysis mediates between the universal structure and the existential realization and enables him to seize intact the concrete living personal existence, without any division of theory and practice; but it has the effect of seeming to give a moral meaning to what is intended to be simply factual. Until personal existence is resolved in steadfast adherence to its existence in the world for death, it has no unity or totality; there is, properly speaking, no subject to seize and interpret. What, then, is the meaning of the resolved personal existence? The clue is found in the nature of temporality.

As all objects do not merely exist in space but are in part constituted by their place in the world (the brake is on the wheel which is on the road which joins the places, etc.), so also they do not merely exist in time but are constituted by a time process: the hoe has been made and will be used for hoeing and is at present lying there in the tool-shed. Even the hoe is not a fully constituted hoe merely existing in time understood as a structureless but irreversible succession of 'nows'; it is not a hoe if it has not been made and it is not a hoe if it will not be used for hoeing, and in this sense it is constituted in time and bears in its essence a reference to the past and the future. The undifferentiated stream of instants would be dateless, but every now is the time for our concerns: now after the morning's work it is time to have lunch, and then there will be time for a rest until it is time for that appointment. But even this time for our concerns is a succession of presents, for there is always something present which indicates that it is now the time for something, by which the past and future are determined as extended backwards or forwards. The absolute, although finite, temporal process is realized in the resolved personal existence, for then the three phases of the process, past, present, and future, which rigidly exclude one another, are constantly held in the indissolubility of their union in interpenetration: structurally, the resolved personal existence assumes and wills continuously and concretely in its immediate preoccupations and projects its having been found already cast into the world and its ultimate death. Its constitution as Care (being detached from itself as possibility, being already cast into the world to die, being bound up with a present everyday existence) shows this structure, and the resolve to interpret the past and determine the present by the ultimate possibility of the future, by treating as nothing the steps which it takes from nothing to nothing, holds the structure together by individual activity and achieves the unity and totality of personal existence as a temporal process. I am myself temporal, not a being who exists in time. I am not a pure presence of a self to itself, but a being who is always already cast into the world (not master of itself and tied in a thousand ways to the not-self) and always already projected in advance of itself, to be realized. This past and this future are external, phases of the temporal process by which I realize myself, and they are also internal because they are both perpetually re-created in the present through my constant acceptance and resolved active willing of my dereliction and death, the two poles of my nothingness. It is in this sense that personal existence is *lumen naturale*, its own light, it has access to its own externality: neither the past nor the future is wholly external to me for they constitute my present, my finite situation; they constitute me in so far as I resolve my whole existence into the will to be what I will be, and I constitute them in the structure of my being and in my activity. Public time measured by clocks is the time for my concerns, and is the necessary condition of there being the world I know, but the temporal structure of personal existence is the necessary condition of there being the I to know. Not only is it the necessary condition, the actual achievement of the I in the resolved existence is temporal, and this I to which the world is fully disclosed gives it a temporal meaning, for its temporality makes it what it is, and makes it nothing: I can only be (as distinct from becoming, in which I never am) by anticipating rigorously what I will be, which is nothing, and repeating what I have been, which is nothing, and recognizing that everything in the world that could ever be present to me is nothing.

Personal existence as a temporal process is historical and makes history. The devaluation of the world accomplished in resolved existence is not a dispensation from active concern; the future sends one back to the present and the past, anticipation of death is a task as well as an interpretation. The resolved existence is concerned to select from the inherited tradition what is repeatable. And it is the business of the historian to disentangle from the actual what is universal, the possible, the repeatable. He cannot do this if he is himself dispersed in the inauthentic existence of everyday, he can only do it if he is himself resolved and living actively in the present as well as actively re-living the past. History is thus only objective in being subjective: it is a specific product of a man oriented towards the future.

This meaning which a resolved personal existence gives to itself and to the world transcends the intelligible world of everyday meanings as this in turn transcends brute existence. I am always already in the world, immersed in my preoccupations, engaged in my projects, realizing my possibilities, and whether I am living authentically or inauthentically, in virtue simply of the self-projection of personal existence, its existence as possibility and not accomplished fact, I am giving meaning to brute existence, my own and that of all things for which I find a use, which I handle or produce, or which I bring into a perspective of interest. In this way, going beyond the actual existents with which I have to do and beyond my own projects in which I am engaged, I posit the world as the totality of all existents, and at the same time and in the same act I posit myself for whom this world exists as in principle able to find access to all these existents and able in principle to find a place for them in the system of uses and meanings which I constitute in living and realizing my possibilities. I am thus capable of being affected by all existents: All existents are in principle relevant to my interests, in my world. I give myself the task in constituting myself and the world of bringing the actual existents into their proper places in my system of uses and meanings. My virtual inclusion of them has to be actualized. It is not a dream world nor a world finished and given, but a brute existence in which personal existence participates and upon which it constitutes an intelligible world answerable to its own possibilities. It is within the limits of this world which I constitute by the basic act of transcendence that I can raise intelligible questions, ask why. *Dasein* itself, the mode of existence of the human being, which is thus the source of all possible questions, is not open to question: it is merely what it is found to be, its temporal structure as Care is ultimate.

This primordial act of transcendence by which I constitute myself and the world in principle is the foundation of all foundations, practical and theoretic: it is the necessity of my being (I do it in living in the midst of what is, it is rooted in my practice and my feeling, it is not intellectual, it is at bottom a total response, as in joy or ennui) and it is my liberty (I am such that I can separate myself from what I am, my being is in question). The brute existence which my activities and projects constitute an intelligible world remains in itself impenetrable, a night, out of which I came, to which I return, and which I taste with nausea if ever I lose the intelligibility and value which personal existence alone can give to brute existence in constituting a world. The experience of nausea, of worthlessness, of absurdity, which sometimes takes me unawares simply proves that it is personal existence which constitutes meanings and an intelligible world, and bears witness to the impenetrable otherness of brute existence which subtends the construction of the intelligible world.

This foundation of all foundations which gives me the task of actually comprehending all existents in the world it posits, founds not only my economic activities, dealing systematically with the useful, and the special perspectives elaborated by the sciences, but also philosophy, politics, and the arts. This complex of activities creates a local world, a particular civilization, a concrete and temporary form of the abstract universal idea of the world which I posit in the act of transcendence.

II

Has Heidegger in the published first part of *Sein und Zeit* on which the foregoing exposition has been based dug away the ground on which he proposed to construct a metaphysic of Being? His description shows the intelligible world of meanings constituted by the structure of personal existence upon the given actuality of brute existence. These meanings answer the questions *what*, *what for*, *how*, *as*, but actuality remains impenetrable to the probe of *why*, as does personal existence itself. Man constitutes meanings but not natures. Therefore there seems to be no possibility of answering the question, *why is what is?* of finding a ground of necessity for all existence, which was the early enterprise of metaphysics in raising the question of Being. *Sein und Zeit* shows man in the midst of all beings in the whole, a situation which both gives rise to and excludes the possibility of metaphysics, since our standing off from things (including ourselves) raises the question and yet our standpoint remains within the whole and excludes in principle an absolute comprehension.

Nevertheless, *Sein und Zeit* as published is only the first part of what Heidegger intended to say, and it has to be interpreted, and indeed revised, in the light of what he has published since. This effaces many of the impressions which that work taken by itself is bound to make. His philosophy takes shape as the historical quest for Being, and is seen to be essentially religious. It no longer looks like a fixed heroic gesture of man permanently caught in the despair of nihilism, and it loses its sensationally dramatic form. True, God is dead, as Nietzsche put it, but the very lack of God is a revelation and a promise.

As Heidegger characteristically puts it in his interpretation of the poet Hölderlin, the time is a time of need because it lies under a double negation, the no-more of the gods that have fled and the not-yet of the god that is coming. The coming of the new god cannot be forced, and a return to any of the old gods is a futile attempt to live in the past. Heidegger seems to think of the self-revelation of Being as a historical development, demanding the appropriate approach and attitude in each phase. The present phase is post-theological and post-metaphysical: it is with the recognition that God is dead and that man has no standpoint outside the totality of things that man must approach again in this age the problem of Being.

Some of Heidegger's later writings (the most important for understanding his thought) are oracular in tone and one can have no confidence in interpreting the cryptic sentences in which his thought is condensed. The attempt here is to present the spirit and orientation of his thought rather than the actual concepts.

To return to the central analysis of *Sein und Zeit:* transcending the primordial act of transcendence which founds the construction of the intelligible world is the act by which the person roused by conscience recognizes in dread the nothing out of which he came and into which he goes and therefore resolves his existence into the nothing which it is by an act of total renunciation. This is held to be not a moral act but the act of integration necessitated by the temporal structure of personal existence, or rather by its total structure as Care. It is enacted on the plane of the quest for Being. In what sense can it be taken to be anything other than complete nihilism? The clue to Heidegger's answer is in his notion of Nothing, the subject of his inaugural lecture at Freiburg.

Nothing is not merely a notional negation, not-anything, and thus the counter-concept opposed to Being; it can be experienced and is itself the source of all forms of negation and negativity. Dread is the experience of Nothing. What happens? The intelligible world constructed by personal existence, in which man feels safe and at home, the world of meanings, is nihilated and he is plunged back into the sheer 'is-ness' of what is, his ship on which he is riding and voyaging disappears in the night and he finds himself in the deep waters and tastes their saltness. This is an experience of brute existence denuded of meanings, the high-tension power of raw actuality; it uncovers the marvellousness of pure 'is-ness', contingency, which reason covers up, and is therefore a revelation of Being, and renews the wonder of philosophy and gives a new impulse to the *why* of science. Nothing does not cancel Being but familiar forms of Being, and therefore puts Being again in question. When the first pre-Socratic thinker asked the question, What is what is? he inaugurated civilization, because of the transcendence which was implied and which has founded the vast complex of meanings and activities which make the historical intelligible world. But the original intensity and comprehensiveness of that question, which made it an experience of marvellousness, has been buried in oblivion by the building up of the intelligible world through the successful uncovering of what-is. Thus knowledge and all the works of man by their very achievement in uncovering what-is and mastering nature have also, and necessarily, at the same time covered up Being and wandered from the point of view from which Being can be glimpsed. Knowledge is in its very validity a form of untruth because it conceals the ignorance which it does not abolish. The openness which alone makes science possible is itself closed, or partially closed, by science, and this increasingly as practical problems are solved with brilliant success which gives a technical bias to human interests, and as pure science moves further from the face of things and becomes more completely abstract and mathematical. Kierkegaard had taken a philosophical stand against the modern multiplication of knowledge, and had sought to return to first things by stressing the *how* at the expense of the *what* and by making a supreme ethical decision the criterion of relevance. Heidegger does it within the tradition of Western philosophy by raising again the question of Being in a way that is intended to break the present preoccupation with technical problems and pursuits and the present pretensions of science, and to renew Western civilization, including its science, by restoring its contact with its source and informing principle in the question which first inspired it and still rules, whether acknowledged or not.

The experience of Nothing, then, is an eclipse of the intelligible world and a precipitation into what-is, which recovers the pristine wonder which first raised the question about Being. But Being is not what-is, brute existence, any more than it is the intelligible world. Nor is it the ground of the world, nor God. Conceptualization fails, but here again the notion of Nothing serves. In the act of transcendence by which personal existence separates itself from what-is and even from its own brute existence and its solidified past, its freedom and its affirmative and originative force lie in its nothingness, and it is then close to Being. This separation from brute existence and from the intelligible world and from one's own past, followed by willed identification with one's situation and assumption of one's past and one's fate, followed by realization of one's possibilities in the world, and again by a separation from this which devalues it and counts it as nothing, this is a mode of conjugation of subject and object expressing a total response of man in a total alertness and openness to Being. Heidegger seems to think of the total renunciation of the resolved personal existence described in *Sein und Zeit*, steadfastly nullifying all realizations without refusing them, as in its perfected purposelessness a form of purification which draws close to Being and, as it were, makes way for Being, by making oneself wholly over to Being: one is serene and listens to the silent voice of Being and bears witness in the world to Being. What seems to be indicated is that this is the appropriate approach at this historical time; this meets the need of the age, the age which is the no-more and the not-yet of the gods, the age when the meaning of the question of Being has been so completely concealed by knowledge and lost sight of in the perspectives of an active civilization that it does not make sense any more. More concretely, he is encouraging those attitudes and points of view which make it possible to recover the original manifest *whatness* of things in contrast to their reductive analysis and exploitation, and to experience the poetry of things in their immediacy without seeing them first in their everyday common sense matter of factness. Being is near, and yet, since it must be sought after and can never be fully nor finally possessed, it is far off. It is by identifying ourselves and attaching ourselves, and by our full awareness and openness, that we keep close to Being.

III

Heidegger's philosophy invites close comparison with the philosophy of Jaspers. At the outset, they seem formally opposed in that Heidegger sets out to explore the structure of Being, whereas Jaspers declares that Being is split into discontinuities which can be surmounted only in living, and that it is naïve still to look for a general homogeneous structure which can be elucidated by thought. In the sequel and full scope of their philosophies the opposition on this score disappears, for both use their descriptions of personal existence to indicate a transcendent Being-in-itself which can be experienced. Nevertheless, the difference in their handling of practically the same descriptive elements is striking. Jaspers gives us a world of bounded situations in which frustration is insurmountable, a world of riddles and final ambiguities, a world in which the closed circuit of objective thought is sealed off in self-contained partial intelligibility, functionally incapable of grasping any possible ultimate of experience, a world, therefore, which throws the individual back on himself with a choice between faith and despair. For Heidegger, there is no ambiguity: the demonstrable structure of personal existence and of the humanly intelligible world shows that it is nothing, and this demonstration is intended to be rigorously objective and binding. All the same, the effect of this analysis might be, as with Jaspers, to throw the existing individual back on himself and lead him into an experience of Being initiated by metaphysical faith. In a sense it is, but Heidegger's way of doing it is more in the spirit of Husserl, and even of Hegel, than in Kierkegaard's. His analysis leads to raising again the question of Being in a new and radical way, for it cuts off the question from all possibility of an answer in terms hitherto used in the history of metaphysics (Will, Idea, etc.); the meanings constituted by the perspectives of science and the perspectives of human projects in the humanly intelligible world have to be surpassed, and the question leads to their being surpassed if we penetrate behind it to the fundamental plane and ask why the question has been raised and why the traditional answers have been given. Why must we ask about the meaning of Being? This becomes the primordial question of philosophy: the question about Being must not be dismissed with the traditional answers which are seen to be no longer possible, it must be probed and penetrated—and this is a new impulse, a renewed initiative in philosophy. If one asks what kind of answer there can be to the question re-opened on this level, that is to emasculate the question and dress it in rhetoric, for the answer is generated by the philosophic vitality of the question and cannot be anticipated. But Heidegger is enfolded by his sense of working within the tradition of Western philosophy and in his re-handling of its most radical question there is an idea of a historical self-revelation of Being, an echo of Hegel less audible in Jaspers.

All this in Heidegger is built on that element in his description of personal existence which has no parallel in Jaspers, viz., the resolution of personal existence in a choice of death as the capital possibility informing all other possibilities, treated as the necessary structure of personal existence without which it simply dissolves. In this description, personal existence is an objective world structure into which the empirical individual is inserted, perhaps another Hegelian trait. At any rate, in this essentially formal treatment of an essentially Kierkegaardian theme Heidegger's disavowal of existentialism seems to be justified. But it is just this part of his analysis which seems impossible to justify.

Kierkegaard in choosing the infinite chose infinite resignation of the finite world; he also recognized that personal existence simply vanishes unless it is stabilized and consolidated in radical and sustained acts of choice. He deliberately refrained from uniting the formal principle of absolute choice with his own material choice in a universal, although the inevitability of choosing the infinite, with all its consequences, was never far from his thoughts. And in respect to death in its explicitness, he occupied himself with the question of relating it to the entire life of the subject and of taking this as the task of life to realize it existentially. There is a long discussion of the question in the chapter 'The Task of Becoming Subjective' in

107

Concluding Unscientific Postscript, from which the following passage is quoted.

'We wish to know how the conception of death will transform a man's entire life, when in order to think its uncertainty he has to think it in every moment, so as to prepare himself for it. We wish to know what it means to prepare for death, since here again one must distinguish between its actual presence and the thought of it. This distinction seems to make all my preparation insignificant, if that which really comes is not that for which I prepared myself; and if it is the same, then my preparation is in its perfection identical with death itself.'

Nevertheless, it is far from being true that Kierkegaard's thought is personally religious and Heidegger's formally philosophic. Behind the rigorous formality of Heidegger's treatment of personal existence it is not difficult to see a quasi-religious purpose at work. The closed objective structure which he makes of personal existence, a universal pattern, by his formal treatment of the choice of death, is not merely used theoretically to cancel the intelligible world and raise the question of Being on another plane; the existential realization of this universal is a life-long task, and personal perfection in purposelessness by means of it is the only way to draw near to Being, to make way for Being, by making oneself wholly over to Being. The question and the answer to the question do not belong to the plane of theoretical philosophy, but to total human experience informed by thinking. Therefore in the profoundest sense Heidegger is an existentialist, and only differs from the others in making the supreme choice demonstrably universal and necessary. The demonstration of course fails, since there is nothing in the temporal structure of personal existence nor in the inevitability and uncertainty of death to constrain a personal choice of death as the only choice which can integrate the temporal phases of an individual existence.

This failure within at the heart of his philosophy, just because of the weight that is put on its structural integrity, reduces the point of putting in question the philosophy as a whole as a critique of the assumptions and pretensions of modern culture. How does Heidegger justify his proposal to restore the primacy and rule of the question of Being? At this time of day, it is seriously asked, does the question of Being make any sense? Heidegger's justification, it may be allowed, is abundantly implicit in his handling of the question throughout, and no other form of justification could be worth half so much. All the same, a greater tenderness with common sense might better serve the cause of 'a guardian of Being'. When it is said that the word Being speaks of the treasure which has been preserved and transmitted in the philosophical tradition, and those who will hear the word are the elect, one seems no longer to be listening to the lucid and persuasive language of that tradition and to have turned back to the oracular obscurity of the pre-Socratics.

VI

JEAN-PAUL SARTRE

(Born 1905)

Everybody who has heard of existentialism without knowing much about it will couple with it the name of Jean-Paul Sartre, who mainly by his novels and plays and as a centre of cult and controversy in Paris has earned notoriety for the movement, so that to many the names of both one and the other are suspect. Nobody who takes the trouble to read Sartre's main work *L'Être et le Néant* carefully will be able either to take the author for a charlatan or the philosophy for a stunt. Sartre is a typical modern French intellectual. The world takes him as such, and dismisses, adores, or reviles him as such. But the adroit omniscience of this French intellectual is founded upon a philosophical keel. He borrows largely from Husserl and Heidegger and profoundly from Hegel, but he handles his themes with professorial sagacity and with a virtuosity all his own. It is no use (English) academic philosophers dismissing him as a mere *littérateur*. In France, philosophers can feel a national pride in this exhibition of French intelligence out-speculating the Germans. In any case, *L'Être et le Néant* is not a mere *tour de force;* for Sartre is supremely in earnest and the argument of the book is the indispensable clue to his life's work.

I

To be conscious is to be conscious of something; consciousness refers to and separates itself from something not itself. And to be conscious of something is to be aware of being conscious of something. But this secondary awareness is implicit in the primary consciousness of something. Otherwise, I should be aware of being conscious of something and aware of being aware of being conscious of something, to infinity. My consciousness cannot become an object to itself in this way; it is seized only as consciousness of something else. Consciousness is always present to something which it is not, and thus is present to itself, but always in the form of not being something. Consciousness comes into the world as a No, and is aware of itself as an everlasting No, as pure possibility separated from everything existent. It is a form of being which implies a form of being other than its own. Itself, it is a mode of being 'which has yet to be what it is, that is to say, which is what it is not and which is not what it is'. On the other hand, the object of consciousness is what it is; it is wholly there, totally given, without any separation from itself; it is not possibility, it is itself, it is in itself; 'uncreated, without any reason, without any relation with another being, being-in-itself has been eternally *de trop*'.

These two modes of being, consciousness and its object, the *pour-soi* and the *en-soi*, are not merely in contrast. Consciousness absolutely requires the given objective world. It only comes into existence as separation from what is there. Consciousness cannot be deduced from the world, which is independent and self-sufficient. The world can be deduced from consciousness; not because consciousness is prior and independent, but because it comes into the world as nothing, as not the world, and gives the world as there. Consciousness is thus relative to the objective world and dependent upon it. On the other hand, consciousness is not something other than the world, since that would be itself an object to consciousness, an *en-soi*, it perpetually reconstitutes itself other than the world, in relation to every item of experience, perpetually puts itself in question, and is thus an absolute. The *en-soi* and the *pour-soi* are therefore modes of being related by an unbridgeable separation. How, then, is knowledge possible, or action, or any form of transcendence? Is Being an irresolvable duality, a plenitude on the one hand and a barren negation on the other, *l'être et le néant?*

If so, how does this remotely resemble our experience of ourselves in the world?

Indeed, it would not be possible to unite the *en-soi* and the *pour-soi* if they were separate entities; and that is the position of defeat in which philosophy stands, whether based like Idealism on the primacy of the *pour-soi* or like Realism on the primacy of the *en-soi*. In order that there can be knowledge and action, and other modes of the conjugation of subject and object, the *pour-soi* must be recognized for what it is: perpetual pure separation and denial, embodied in historical existence in the world, yet not identified with that existence as a property of it nor as its totality, but perpetually reconstituting itself and having a virtual totality of its own. This pure nothing which limits and defines being and is not a property of it nor something else set over against it is not a mere hypothesis to overcome the riddle of philosophy, it falls into place in the description of the only conditions which make our human presence in the world possible. Ontology, description of the structure of Being, will thus describe how consciousness, human presence in the world, neither substance nor process, is related to the body, to its situation in the world, to past, present, and future, to knowing, desiring, willing, and choosing, to having and doing, to value and ideals, to other consciousness. By its convincing description, ontology, disposing of baffling problems in philosophy which have made the wearisome circuit of idealism-realism, will reveal the truth of the human situation and lay the foundations for ethics, prescriptions for living.

II

Consciousness, then, comes into existence as consciousness of something with awareness of this consciousness. Always the *pour-soi* comes into existence by separation from, that is dependence upon, some matter of fact which merely is. I am conscious of being a waiter because I am not wholly and solely a waiter, but I happen to get my existence by separation from (or trying to be) a waiter, not a journalist nor a diplomat. I am only a *pour-soi* by being an *en-soi* which I am not; but I am not merely not this *en-soi*, nor merely dependent upon it for another form of existence (as a foil), I try to take it up into myself, to assimilate it completely, to make it wholly my consciousness of myself without any separation; and this I am never able to do. This contingency of the *pour-soi*, its dependence upon the *en-soi*, is its facticity. It can never found itself, it can only found its own nothingness by relation to the *en-soi* which is gratuitously given, just what it is. Man is not a substance that thinks, but a separation from all substance: I am not, therefore I think. But the separation is never complete, for it is separation from a contingent substance which is not merely its occasion but also its mode and instrument: this is its facticity.

In its nature, then, consciousness by being always consciousness of something refers to itself and constitutes itself apart as not something else. This distinction, being consciousness aware of itself and not a distinction made by an onlooker (as between that inkstand and the pen), already constitutes the consciousness as personal, for personality in the first place is being which exists for itself in the sense of being present to itself. But this consciousness is consciousness not merely of difference but also of the nature of the difference, a perception however rudimentary of the object as a plenitude and of itself as a lack. My consciousness of myself thus already implies a projection of myself towards my possibility, what I lack in order to be myself identified with myself; and this is the structure of desire and the movement towards fulfilment. The ideal project which defines our existence and is the meaning of human presence in the world is the nisus towards some form of unity of the *pour-soi* with the *en-soi* in a totality which saves both. That is in principle impossible. Man aspires to be god, but god is a self-contradiction. Nevertheless, this absolute value is the lure which governs our lives.

The *pour-soi* since it constitutes itself by separating itself from that to which it is present can only exist historically, that is, in the temporal mode. It is always present, but it has a past and a future, by which it generates a self and a world. I am not the *en-soi* I am present to, and I am not the *en-soi* that I leave behind. Nevertheless, it is my being and not another's that I leave behind: my past is my facticity. I am angry, an official, unhappy: I transcend these conditions in my awareness of them and they are thus separated from me as my past, but in leaving them behind they remain and haunt me. The past is the totality always growing of the *en-soi* which we are. But whilst we live we are never identified with it. It is not what I am but what I was. I am totally responsible for it and cannot change its content, but I can interpret it, give it a sequel which will alter its meaning; until in the end I become my own past finally, fixed and solidified, open without defence to the judgement of others, an *en-soi*. Meanwhile, I happen to be sad or a waiter, but it is only by separating myself from some condition that I *am*. The past is the inverse of value, of the human ideal, for it is the *pour-soi* congealed in the *en-soi*. That is why the past can be idealized, for it seems to be wholly given and solely what it is and at the same time human. The future is constituted by the lack which the *pour-soi* is; it is open, problematical, essentially a project. Thus there is not first a universal time-stream in which the *pour-soi* suddenly appears without a past. The phenomenal world comes into existence with the birth of the *pour-soi*, which from the moment when it constitutes itself by separating itself from the *en-soi* has a past, the *en-soi* refused. Thus appears a world with a past and a future as the mode of being of the *pour-soi*. But in this mode of temporality it never is nor can be wholly and solely itself, coincidence with itself. In aspiring to this absolute repose in himself, coincidence with himself, man aspires (vainly) to an intemporal mode of being.

III

Consciousness, the *pour-soi*, transcends the world and is not itself a phenomenon, given as an appearance. The objects of consciousness, phenomena, the appearances of things, disclose what is really there as it really is, but never exhaustively. The *en-soi* given to consciousness in phenomena is being in its plenitude, and the source of all being. Consciousness implies and refers to an existence other than its own and to its own existence as a question. It is this relation of the *pour-soi* to the *en-soi* which is the foundation (and only condition) of knowledge and action. Knowledge is necessarily intuition, the presence of consciousness to the object which it is not. This is the original condition of all experience. Before the object is defined and interpreted, consciousness constitutes itself by separating itself from it. Consciousness does not separate the thing from itself as being not itself, which could only be done by a third-party and if consciousness were itself an *en-soi*. Consciousness is only aware that it is itself not-that, and this is the first phase of knowledge and of action. 'The *pour-soi* is a being for whom his being is in question in his being inasmuch as this being is a certain manner of *not-being* a being which he posits at the same stroke as other than he.' Thus knowledge is not in any sense a relation into which two beings enter. It is the very being of the *pour-soi* inasmuch as it is presence to . . . that is to say, inasmuch as it has to be its being by making itself not be a certain being to which it is present. Thus the formula is: 'the fundamental relation by which the *pour-soi* has to be as not being *this* particular being to which it is present is the foundation of all knowledge of this being'. There is neither continuity nor discontinuity between knower and known; the relation is unmediated identity, denied. There is an image of it if one imagines two curves which touch at a point with a common tangent. If the curves are covered up so that one sees only the coincidence of the curves at their point of common tangency, it is one and the same line, separated by nothing, neither continuous nor discontinuous, but identical. Uncover the two curves, and they are seized at once as two and distinct, even at the point of tangency. There has been no physical separation, but the two movements with which we draw the curves in order to perceive them involve a negation, a separation, as the act which constitutes each. The internal negation which constitutes consciousness and is the condition of knowledge is a special case of negation since it does not affirm a separation between two pre-existing things having their own character and being *en-soi*. The *pour-soi* is itself characterized only as not *this en-soi*. It reveals the world in being not the world and makes it that there is a world, but adds nothing to it. The *pour-soi* does not only start from *this-here* as given and constitute itself by a negation (I am not that), for the same negation constitutes thishere and that-there, and the whole world besides which is virtually there as the ground and as the totality of all future and all possible negations, corresponding to the unrealized totality of the *pour-soi*. The *pour-soi* as co-present to the particular object and the totality spatializes the world and characterizes itself as not extended: each particular *en-soi* has its place and the *pour-soi* is present to it without place (I may be conscious of the absent).

A thing is what it is, its qualities are neither subjective nor synthesized in it: a green cone is not first a cone, then green. It is entirely what appears to consciousness, since consciousness is nothing in itself and cannot act upon it, but consciousness has always a perspective view and does not attend to all aspects at once. A particular act of self-realization which constitutes the *pour-soi* is always a negation of some quality of the object in the way of seizing it, say the greenness rather than the conicality, which leaves to the future a difference of emphasis. The instantaneous negation of the *en-soi* by the *pour-soi* is bound, as to its complement, to the immediate negation of the *pour-soi* by itself: its past solidifies into an *en-soi*, its future possibilities draw it on to the realization of the being it aspires to be. The negation is thus an engagement constituting different futures, the different potentialities of the two types of being—future states of the world and future possibilities of self-realization. The negation of this-here by me, which is immediately left behind as my past because I separate myself at once from what I am, involves my own future and the future of the world. Unreflectively, I am not aware of my own lack (as pure negation, nothingness), but only of the incompleteness of the object. I must go on to know it in its essence as other than I. But its essence is identical with its existence, and thus I will and desire the concrete universal of past, present, and future states of the world, with which to be united. This is out of reach. I experience beauty as a lack. This reference of the particular thing to what is beyond itself, other states of itself and other things, comes home to the *pour-soi* in a call to action; for the world is a world of tasks and it is the nature of things to be bound together as means and ends: things are both things and tools, not first one in order to become the other but always under the double aspect. To be in the world is not to escape from the world towards oneself but to escape from the world towards a beyond which is the future of the world. The complex of tool-things does not refer to and end finally in the *pour-soi* (as Heidegger says); the totality of this complex is the exact correlative of my possibilities. And, as I am my possibilities, the order of tool-things in the world is the image projected in the *en-soi* of my possibilities, that is to say, of what I am. But this is an image I can never decipher; I adapt myself to it in and by action: I am inserted without recourse inside the circuit means-ends.

The ideal of knowledge is to know the thing as it is in itself. But this would be possible only if consciousness could identify itself with the thing, and then there could no longer be consciousness and the possibility of knowledge. Thus knowledge is not relative in the Kantian sense of not being able to know the thing as it is in itself (as though this were a possible notion of knowledge), but simply in the sense that it is wholly human, that is, the separation of a consciousness which brings into existence a world, Being as known. Knowledge puts us in the presence of the absolute, what is there, and has its truth: what is truly known is nothing other than the absolute, but the knowledge is strictly human and could not be otherwise.

Since the body and the senses are themselves first objects of knowledge, it would be quite improper to treat them in an ontological description as the ground or meaning of knowledge. We know the bodies of others, and my body is known by another. Thus the body involves the existence of others and our relation to others.

IV

Neither idealism nor realism has been able to give an intelligible account of my relation to another, and thus to refute solipsism. It is not primarily a relation of knowledge, and it is because they have treated it as such that these philosophies have condemned themselves to fail. Heidegger comes nearest to success, but because (although a pupil of Husserl) he does not start from the *cogito* (the deduction of the world from a subject who brings himself into existence by detaching himself from it as given) he cannot account for the concrete individual whom I know and slips back into idealism, taking others as given along with me inserted in the complex of tools. I cannot be an object to myself; and the other as a subject cannot be an object to me either. He escapes my consciousness as knowledge altogether— in principle. I experience him as a subject not when I see him as an object and infer from his appearance that he is a person like myself, but when he sees me as an object. Then I am sucked into his orbit. My world dissolves and flows away from me and is re-constituted by and about him. I become an item in his world, an item and a world for ever inaccessible to me. When I fall under the regard of another a haemorrhage sets in, my world leaks and flows away: I am wholly given in my appearance to the other, like an *en-soi*. The other is, in principle, the one who looks at me not the one at whom I look—a subject not an object. If I am caught unawares immersed in an activity of which I become ashamed on being discovered (spying through a keyhole, let us say), I become conscious not of myself but of myself as existing for another. This is an inaccessible dimension of myself. I am not only the being I was (my own *en-soi*, my facticity) and the being I have to be (my possibility) but also the being I am to another. I discover that my liberty is limited by his, that I have an outside which I can never see that gives me a totality that belongs only to the human being whose life is accomplished and finished, whose possibilities are no more. Under the regard of another, I am lost, a being I cannot know, placed I cannot know where, in a world that is not mine: yet this is veritably me, as much as the person I was or the person I am yet to be. This is what happens to me when I am the object of another's regard and he organizes me in his world. This relationship is not an objective relation between bodies in the world, it is not a relationship within the world at all: my transcendence is transcended, I experience concrete proof of another's transcendence, a beyond the world. In this experience, solipsism is not merely refuted, but shattered: under the regard of another, I experience my own objectivity and in that I experience the subjectivity of another—in the destruction of my own—as I never can whilst I remain a subject and he an object to me. That I am an object for another subject is as indubitable as that I exist for myself, and certain forms of consciousness (for example, shame) can only come to me in that way.

The other is a consciousness, a *pour-soi*, a personal being, a self, like me. I should be identified with the other were it not that I constitute myself by dissociation from the other *pour-soi* as from the *en-soi* (and from myself). But this dissociation is mutual and is the attempt to constitute oneself a subject by constituting the other an object. We refuse to be each other. This double negation destroys the objectivity of one or the other: both cannot be at the same time objects for each other. The other as a subject not myself escapes me. I do not seize him directly, but by not being the objective me whom he separates himself from to constitute himself a subject: I refuse myself refused. But to do this is to recognize both the other and my objectivity for the other. This acceptance (in refusal) of my objectivity for the other is the price of my not being the other. My alienated refused self which the other separates himself from in making himself a subject conscious of me and which I separate myself from in striving to be a subject and tearing myself from the other, has to be accepted or else both the other and I disappear. I escape from the other in leaving my alienated self (my self for him) in his hands. My detachment from the other which constitutes myself is in its structure an assumption as mine of this me which the other separates himself from as his object: it is *only* that. The me, alienated and refused (from which both dissociate ourselves to constitute ourselves independent persons), is at the same time my bond with the other and the symbol of our absolute separation. The separation of the other and myself is never something given, like the separation of two bodies in the world for a third person. In affirming myself, I accept myself as object for the other, but I cannot know this alienated self which is constituted by the other's dissociation: it is my outside, really a dimension of my being, and not an image of me in the consciousness of the other. I am to myself unlimited, pure possibility, for ever not-this; but to the other, seen from the outside, I am limited. My being-for-another is neither *en-soi* nor *pour-soi*, but a being torn to pieces between two negations: the other constitutes himself as not this me of whom he has the intuition, and I have no intuition of this me which I am. However, this me produced by the one and assumed by the other gets an absolute reality from being the sole possible separation between two beings fundamentally identical in their mode of being and immediately present one to the other, for consciousness alone can limit consciousness. On the basis of this acceptance of my limit, obscuring it, comes of course my limitation of the other. It is in fear, shame, pride, vanity, and the like that we experience our existence for others, and these affective states indicate how in practice we pass from one condition to the other, sometimes transcended, sometimes transcending.

What is the other as an object for me? A concrete centre about which a total world is organized, but contemplated and placed within my world, a transcendence transcended, an enclave within my sovereign territory. In principle, I can interpret correctly and know exhaustively the other as object; and nothing in his objectivity refers to his subjectivity which is in principle beyond knowledge and out of the world—and is nothing. When the other as subject arises, the other as object is shattered—the one does not refer to the other nor manifest the other. The other as object (because it can be transformed into subject) is a highly dangerous explosive and my efforts are always concentrated on taking care that it does not go off. But I cannot control this and I can never reconcile the two aspects of the other nor reject either. Only the dead are permanently objective.

The body is a concrete centre of reference. The things in the world are oriented towards the body and reveal it. All the things which I habitually use are organized in my world and indicate my bodily presence which gives them their place and their meaning. Similarly, the great public places and services presuppose and refer to the bodies that frequent and use them; the world is organized and routed for prescribed uses. Objects are both things and tools, given to sensation and use. In a world of serviceable-things, sensation and action cannot properly be distinguished. Thus inquiry should not start with the body as given and ask how we come to act in and know the world, for with the emergence of the *pour-soi* in relation to the world the world itself as a complex of serviceable-things reveals to us our bodies. I objectify my own body and senses by taking them from my observation of the senses and bodies of others, or from my objective knowledge; I then think of myself as looking on at my own body and sense operations. But that would involve my power to look on at myself looking on, etc., to infinity. The fact is I am my senses and my body and cannot make them an object to myself, for in attempting to do so I am identified with them: the eye whilst it is looking does not see itself. My body is not for me a tool inserted in the complex of tools, but is of such a nature that it can both fit into the complex of tools and be a last term, not itself a tool, which makes sense and order of all. My body is both a point of view and a starting point, for it organizes and fixes the world which I transcend towards a new order by action which realizes other possibilities. It is also an obstacle, a resistance to my projects, with its own 'coefficient of adversity'. It is the condition of action, that is of choice, as of the world of perception.

But as a point of view, my body is not a point of view on which I can take another point of view, just as it is not an instrument which I can use by means of another instrument. I live my body: I do not (cannot) use it, as I cannot transcend and know it. In immediate experience I am not explicitly conscious of it; it is itself passed over as a sign is passed over in making use of the signification, for example, a word or phrase in seizing its meaning. I am conscious of it sideways and retrospectively as of something radically contingent which I cannot seize.

To be conscious is always to be conscious of something against the background of the world, and is always a bodily consciousness, visual or other, against the complete sensory consciousness of the world. Thus in simple consciousness of something, consciousnessness is aware in different fashion of the total world and of the total body. This consciousness of the body is affective not cognitive, coenaesthetic. It may be painful, agreeable, or without feeling tone, a pure apprehension of one's contingent existence. When it is painful it is my effort to get away from it, to project myself beyond it that brings it into consciousness. But when it is not painful, it may be no less unpleasant, for it is then that we are seized by that nausea which may be worse than painful consciousness. This primal nausea is no metaphor, it is the real thing, the reaction to our sense of pure contingency, which is the root of all other physical vomiting which is, so to speak, a reminiscence of it.

In brief, the body *for me* is both the centre of reference indicated by the serviceable-things organized in the world and the pure contingency lived by the *pour-soi*. The body of another person to which the serviceable-things of the world refer as to me, indicating a common world, differs from mine simply as being a possible tool and as a body on which I can take a point of view. My perception of another is radically different from my perception of things because I see him in the setting of some piece of his own world: it is always more than a body I see, for it is a transcendence in time and space.

Thus the body exists in three modes or dimensions. I live my body; my body is known and used by another; in so far as I am an object for another, he is a subject for me and I exist for myself as known by another as a body.

V

The *pour-soi*, being related to the other in this way either as subject or as object, tries to escape becoming an object to the other, strives to assimilate the other or to make the other the object, engages in love or hate. In love, it is the liberty of the other that I want to assimilate or to possess as liberty; for it is the liberty of the other that separates the other from me and constitutes me an object revealing my outside to the other. In loving, I demand that the one I love shall exist solely to choose me as an object, and thus be the origin of my existence for another: it is this alone that gives me an existence not merely *de facto* (*de trop*) but *de jure*, willed by the entire liberty of another, whose existence I will with my own liberty. If I can possess the will of another to whom I am an object, an essence, without infringing its liberty, I become my own foundation and justification. But in order to be loved in this fashion the lover has to make himself an object capable of seducing the loved one, an object that can stand in place of the whole world and be worth the whole world, and here it is the language that the lover employs that promises best to serve his interests; but he can no more know how his language will be taken and interpreted by the loved one than he can know how his body and himself will be taken; his language too has an outside inaccessible to him. He will never begin to succeed until he makes the loved one himself wish and demand to be loved absolutely in the same fashion. For the other can never love me as an object, and he can love me as a subject only by making himself an object which will be all the world to me and seduce me. The loved one only becomes lover by becoming consumed with the desire to be loved. Thus each is trying to be an object of fascination to the other and to demand that the other exist solely to found, will, and sustain him as object. To love is in its essence the project to make oneself loved. The aim is balked quite inevitably. To gain his end, the lover would have to reduce the world to the loved one and himself and have the other exist solely to found his objectivity, and thus give him security and *raison d'être* in his subjectivity; and he would be for the other supreme value and all the world. It is in principle that this enterprise is doomed, for I cannot be loved like this as an object, and I cannot be other than an object to another, and the love of the other is essentially the same project to be loved as subject by me. I cannot get to the goal, I can only turn aside to masochism, making myself wholly an object, using my liberty to deprive myself of liberty, or to sadism, compelling the other to become wholly a thing, a body. These aberrations are themselves self-defeating. And they are only isolated and developed moments of normal sexual intercourse, which is the original project for possessing the liberty of the other through his objectivity. For sexual differentiation and sexual acts spring from deeper ontological structures. The desire which attempts to satisfy itself in sexual acts is a desire for a person taken in his life and place and to become with that person nothing other than one's flesh and blood, pure facticity, contingency. I make myself flesh in the presence of the other in order to appropriate the flesh of the other. The ideal end of desire is the complete incarnation of both consciousnesses in the embrace, with the elimination of movement, the world, even of consciousness. It is the choice of a mode of consciousness: why does the consciousness choose to annul itself under the form of desire? In desire I live my body in a special manner and the world about me suffers a modification: my body is no longer felt as the instrument which cannot be used by another instrument, corresponding to my acts and to a world of serviceable-things; it is lived as flesh, and it is in reference to my flesh that I apprehend the world about me: I make myself passive, I am more sensible of the material substance of things than of their form and use: consciousness sinks into a body which sinks into the world. I come very near to being a thing in the middle of the world, and very like the dead. The meaning of all this is in the attempt to seize the liberty of the other in itself by reducing it to identity with the palpable. This ideal aim is inevitably frustrated by turning into mere power over the body of the other. I wish to be drunk by my body as the ink by a drunkard in order that the other shall do likewise. The consummation of the sexual act disturbs the profounder intention, which anyhow is doomed to frustration since it is self-contradictory. The liberty, subjectivity, of the other cannot be seized physically.

Obviously, the possible attitudes towards the other cannot be all reduced to these variations on the sexual theme; but all the complex behaviour of men one towards another is only elaboration of these two attitudes, love and desire, and of hate. Certainly, particular forms of behaviour (collaboration, struggle, rivalry, emulation, submission, pity, shame, etc.) are infinitely more delicate to describe, for they depend on the actual situations and concrete detail of each relation of the *pour-soi* with the other, but they all enclose within them as their skeleton the sexual relations, simply because these attitudes are the fundamental projects by which the *pour-soi* realizes its being-for-another and tries to transcend this factual situation. These original attitudes are all doomed to move in a circle of frustration, each evoking and developing another form without ever breaking out or achieving the ideal aim. The other is in principle out of reach. We could take a consistent attitude towards another only if we were revealed *at the same time* as subject and as object, which is in principle impossible. Even an ethic of complete respect for the liberty of the other does not succeed, for it is my existence itself which imposes a limit on the liberty of the other, and any of my projects realizes this limit. To surround the other with tolerance is to force him to live in a tolerant world, and deprives him of the opportunity of developing the virtues and qualities which are demanded by an intolerant world. In education, we choose for others principles and values in which they are brought up, and to choose for them freedom is not less to limit theirs. It is our existence itself (whatever we do) that limits the freedom of the other, and not even suicide can modify that original situation: whatever our actions are, it is in a world where there is already the other and where I am *de trop* in relation to the other that we carry them out. It is in this original situation that the notion of sin, original sin, which has haunted mankind is rooted.

The fact of my self-affirmation makes of the other an object and an instrument, and this original theme only is played with all its variations in all our relations.

I cannot possess the liberty of another, then, and when I am the object of another's regard I may turn my own regard upon him as though two liberties could struggle for supremacy; but when I do so he at once becomes an object for me and loses all the efficacy of a subject that makes me an object. I may carry this attitude through, and reduce all men to objects for me; I may make myself indifferent to them and surround myself with a kind of practical solipsism. I then act as if I were alone in the world, dealing with objects, and functions, and tools. But it is a transparent self-deception from which I am likely sooner or later to be rudely awakened; and even if I am not, the price I pay is to lose all sense of my own objectivity, my reality, and in so far as I manage to retain it I have an uneasy sense of the reality which I am ignoring, an uncomfortable feeling of being everywhere looked at and of being helpless, since, having pretended to myself that I am not observed, I cannot take appropriate defensive action. My double project towards the other is not only frustrated but so obscured that it remains an irritant and a disturbance: on the one hand, I am not protecting myself against the danger of being exposed to the liberty of another; on the other, I am not attempting to use this liberty of the other to complete my own being and give me my own *raison d'être*.

In despair of succeeding by these futile means, the *pour-soi* may seek to get rid of the other by bringing about his death. This is hate. This is a policy of despair, since the *pour-soi* abandons half the project and simply aspires to get rid of its own inaccessible outside. It is the attempt to realize more effectively the mode of indifference, to live alone. In hating one other in this sense I hate not some detestable trait or feature but the offending transcendence of the other, his un-get-at-able subjectivity which makes me an object for him, and in hating this one I hate and wish to destroy all, the general principle of the existence of others. Hatred is a black sentiment because it demands to be disapproved and is contemptuous of the disapproval, and thus aims at defying and destroying the liberty of each other. But even if hate succeeded, it could not get rid of the consciousness of the other, it could not restore the lost innocence of solipsism. The past would haunt me, not for my crime, but as the still effective subjectivity of the other, judging me, making me an object irremediably, a fate as irremediable as my own death. Hate is the last throw of despair, and the retreat from its futility has no escape but to withdraw again into the circle of frustration which it has in vain tried to break out of. [At this point, Sartre inserts the following footnote. 'These considerations do not exclude the possibility of an ethic of salvation. But this salvation must be attained after a radical conversion of which we cannot speak here.']

Of course we find ourselves by the side of others as well as over against them. This experience of the *we*, however, is derivative and not primitive. It can only be understood in terms of the original structure of being-for-another of which it is a complication. The we may be experienced as object or as subject. When any two are engaged in any of the forms which the relation between one and another may take, the appearance of a third transforms the situation, and may do so in various ways, but most frequently by constituting a we or a they, and in any case it is always and necessarily a modification of the primitive structure. Work by the side of others under the eye of an overseer or master is the most radical and the most humiliating experience of the we as object, and in this case the I is closely integrated with the others and the machines in a total mechanical system determined by an end; the machines and the objects manufactured indicate the places and the roles of the operators. But this is merely a case that happens to be favourable to the recognition of the we as object. Any situation can do so none the less. And just as we are conscious of our existence for the other as part of our structure, without actually being under the eye of any other, so we know that the existence of humanity involves the possibility of a plurality of consciousnesses existing for others as object or as subject; but it is only a complication of the original structure: hence, class consciousness and the various phenomena of group structure and social psychology. The experiences and tentatives of the crowd correspond closely to the tentatives in love and desire. And merger in the crowd offers a way of escape to the individual consciousness anxious to forget its irreparable isolation and responsibility, its liberty. Since the we is realized only in relation to others, the realization of humanity as such can only take place by positing the existence of a third, distinguished in principle from humanity, in whose eyes humanity is constituted an object. This is simply an ideal concept and corresponds to the idea of God as the being who sees and is not seen. We are always trying to experience our participation in humanity as an object, an historical object working out its destiny, and we never can, since God is the radically absent and there is no experience of a third party for whom humanity as such is an object. Humanity as such has no outside.

Our existence as subjects in common is indicated to us by the world of manufactures and of public signs. The consumer is always in mind to the manufacturer, his liberty, his needs and possibilities. The consumer's ends are generalized and the article on the market indicates the universal we and universal ends. The market reveals to me that I share my transcendence, that I am a one. In using the public services or any common object I am standardized as one of the universal we. The experience is most accented in the rhythm of common action, as in rowing or singing or marching together. But in all cases it is only a psychological experience, never any modification of the fundamental structures of being. In my being-for-another I exist with an outside exposed to the other, in a dimension really and objectively mine. Nothing in the experience of the we alters this or adds anything comparable to it. It may seem that the conflict which derives from the original situation can be deflected or absorbed in the experience of the we as a union of all subjects engaged in making themselves master of the earth. But this is a mere wish, for the subjectivity of the other remains radically separate and inaccessible, and I cannot hope to enter into union with it as it were sideways and inadvertently when in principle it defeats all my efforts and ruses. This experience of the we is partly dependent upon the partial organization of the world as a system of serviceable-things in common, and partly it is a personal and unstable feeling which in certain situations may or may not be the impression which any given person has. The serviceable-things of the world, which indicate my transcendence and occasion experience of the we, are already humanized; they imply the other and would not have for me the meaning they do have unless I had direct experience of the other in my relation to him: they are never primary, nor can they be a substitute for this fundamental relation. The instability of the we experienced as subject is exemplified in the anarchy of the bourgeois class which refuses to recognize its class basis until it becomes an object under judgement and is made to feel fear and shame. There is no way out: the essence of the relations between consciousnesses is not togetherness, it is conflict.

VI

The *pour-soi*, then, comes into existence by separating itself from the *en-soi*, and this is the condition of both knowledge and action; of knowledge because by this separation the objective world is indicated, organized, and explored—in the way that has been shown; of action because by this separation the *pour-soi* founds itself as nothing and seeks to found itself as something, to acquire the unquestionable being of *en-soi*—in a way that has now to be shown. The *pour-soi* not only transcends the world and therefore makes it that there is a world and interprets it, in the way described by Heidegger, it continually changes the world by action upon it, modifying the *en-soi* in its own constitutive material nature (a possibility which raises a metaphysical problem beyond the scope of ontological description). Why does the *pour-soi* act, and what does it mean to act? But knowing and doing are not the most general modes of human living, for knowing is a mode of having. The general modes are having, doing, and being. They are not finally separated modes; for example, a moral agent may act in order to make himself, and make himself in order to be. The present tendency in philosophy follows the tendency in physics to resolve substance into process, into simple movement. The aim of ethics used to be to provide man with a mode of being; for example, this was the aim of the Stoics and of Spinoza. But if the being of man is resolved into the sequence of his acts, morality cannot raise man to a status above his acts, and puts the supreme value of action in the doing, as Kant does. Is the supreme value of human activity in doing or in being, and where does having come in?

We must begin by analysing the notion of action. An act is intentional, or it is not properly speaking an act; it implies a lack that is to be remedied. As such it cannot be motivated from behind, by the past or the state of affairs: it is by an isolation of the state of affairs by a preliminary act of negation (separating the situation as an object), and then by the positing of an end, a difference, by another act of negation, that the past or the present can be interpreted and converted into a motive for action. That is to say, liberty of the agent is the foundation and indispensable condition of all action, liberty as conscious separation from what exists and self-projection towards what is conceived to be possible. The worker does not revolt against the conditions of his life unless and until he can separate himself from them by conceiving and projecting himself towards a better state of things in a realizable future. The motive to act becomes the intention to act and the act moves towards an end in view. This complex is indissolubly one; the terms mutually interpret one another and do not derive simply the one from the other or from any other simple antecedent. Fear may prompt me to act, but only because what I fear to lose is already established as an ideal end for me; and if I reject that end the fear has no more power to move me to act, it becomes a baseless, irrational, unmeaning fear. The single movement of separation from the present and projection towards the future, which is the formal self-constitution of the *pour-soi* (the coming into existence of consciousness), contains motive, act, and end, as its integral parts. The act in this total sense is liberty, and liberty is not a property of human nature but is human existence, the separation in consciousness of the *pour-soi* from the *en-soi*, which is always a particular act.

'To be, for the *pour-soi*, is to cancel the *en-soi* which he is. On these conditions, liberty can be nothing other than this cancellation. It is by this that the *pour-soi* escapes from his being as from his essence, it is by this that he is always something other than what one can *say* of him, for at least he is the one who escapes from this very classification, the one who is already beyond the name one gives him, the attribute one recognizes in him. To say that the *pour-soi* has to be what it is, to say that it is what it is not in not being what it is, to say that in it existence precedes and conditions essence or inversely, according to Hegel's formula, that for it *Wesen ist was gewesen ist*, is to say one and the same thing, namely, that man is free. By the mere fact, indeed, that I am conscious of the motives which solicit my action, these motives are already transcendent objects for my consciousness, they are outside; I should seek in vain to cling to them: I escape from them by my very existence. I am condemned to exist always beyond my essence, beyond the affective and rational motives of my act: I am condemned to be free.' (*L'Être et le Néant*, p. 515.)

This freedom can be masked, but not destroyed; I can deceive myself, but not cease to be free. Thus we tend to think of motives, affective and rational (e.g. fear, health), as constants, given in the world and encountered, coming from God, nature, human nature, or society, in virtue of which the *pour-soi* is given an essence and becomes *en-soi*. This is a dead world, the world of the past. Life and liberty mean separation from whatever is and has been, a projection into the new, and it is this perpetual projection which constitutes motives and ends; they are never given. Human presence in the world is not a form of being, but a form of doing, of choosing and making itself.

'It is entirely abandoned, without any help of any kind, to the insupportable necessity of making itself be down to the least detail. Thus, liberty is not *a* being: it is the being of man, that is to say, his lack of being. If one first conceives of man as a plenum, it would be absurd afterwards to look in him for moments or psychic regions in which he would be free: as well look for space in a vessel which one has previously filled to the brim. Man cannot be sometimes free and sometimes bound: he is entirely and always free or he is not.' (Ibid., p. 516.)

Like motives and ends, will and the passions are not given states of mind, but are constituted like the *pour-soi* itself by separation from what is and projection towards what does not yet exist: they are elements which express and furnish man's freedom, not determinants to which he is subject. The will is not more free than the passions, since it is the *pour-soi* in itself by its self-constitution that projects itself towards an end beyond present existence; the will or deliberation is merely refinement by reflection upon this self-projection, it is self-examination rather than self-determination, for 'when I deliberate, the die is cast'. If I deliberate, that is because it is part of my original project to give myself a rational account of my action before I act. The very satisfaction of the will in its own consummation, 'I have done what I wanted to do', reveals its dependence upon a primary intention at a deeper level, the project to be an '*en-soi–pour-soi*', of which it is one form of attempted realization.

I am a being who is originally pro-ject, that is to say, who defines himself by his end; in being separation from myself (from my facticity) which falls into the past and from the world to which I am present, I am transcendence towards a form of being with which I can be identified, although as transcendence I can never be identified with any form of being. There are a thousand ways of affirming this separation, this transcendence: I can, for example, live my body by identifying myself with it either in its endurances or in its delights, or by ascetic renunciations, or by hypochondriac cultivation; and I can relate myself to my own past and to the things in the world in a similar variety of ways. My original project, my choice of myself, is worked out in choices which are an explication of the original choice. One could choose otherwise in a particular case (say, one could have chosen to go on with the fatigues of an expedition in-instead of giving it up), but only at the cost of a conversion, a change in the original project or choice of myself (becoming, say, an athlete instead of a hypochondriac). *In theory*, any detail of action may be traced back to the original choice, which is nothing other than the way in which the *pour-soi* separates himself from himself and from the world, his way of being-in-the-world. Beyond this it is not possible to go.

This analysis points to the possibility of an existentialist psycho-analysis by which to explain and understand personality and behaviour. It would differ from Freudian psycho-analysis in rejecting determinism by past events in a psyche reacting to the pressure of circumstances. Simply, such an existentialist psycho-analysis would be founded on the basic principle that every gesture and trait of character is to be interpreted by its integration through secondary and primary structures in the total personality, and not as the effect of an antecedent cause in a past psychic state. The inferiority complex is a primary structure in this sense, a free projection of myself as inferior before another; 'it is the way in which I choose to assume my being-for-another, the free solution which I find for the existence of the other, that insurmountable scandal'. I express my whole self, that is to say, the unrealized choice of myself, in the least action, just as I bring the world into organized existence in my perception of the least object. This fundamental act of liberty which I am, by which I constitute myself endlessly, is the choice of myself in the world and at the same time discovery of the world. The consciousness of my original choice is my consciousness of myself. In being conscious, I am separating myself from what I am and from what I am present to, that is, I am choosing how I shall be related to them: 'choice and consciousness are one and the same thing'. My initial and ultimate project is always the rudiment of a solution of the problem of being, not a solution first conceived and then realized, because we *are* that solution and can only apprehend it in living it. Just because we are always wholly present to ourselves, we cannot hope to have an analytical and detailed consciousness of what we are. And in choosing ourselves we interpret the world as the image of what we are: the value of things, the parts they play in my life, my relation to them, sketch the image of me, of my choice.

This initial choice of myself which sketches my solution of the problem of being is always capable of being changed, and it is only such a radical change that will make me act otherwise than as I do. The meaning of the dread which I feel when I realize my liberty is the recognition that my choice could be otherwise, that it is, that I am, *de facto* not *de jure*, and that this choice, which is not justified, which does not derive from anything antecedent, is yet the foundation of all value and all reality for me, all my interpretations. In separating itself from the *en-soi*, itself gratuitous, the *pour-soi* makes itself gratuitous. My ultimate choice, being absolute, unconditioned, is precarious, may be replaced. But since the world is apprehended and interpreted by us by means of and in terms of this fundamental choice we have made, a radical change of this sort, whilst always possible, is in the highest degree difficult and unlikely. Other choice is the choice of others, not easily a possibility for us.

VII

'The decisive argument used by common sense against liberty consists in reminding us of our impotence. Far from being able to modify our situation at will, it seems that we cannot change ourselves. I am not "free" to escape from the lot of my class, my nation, my family, nor even to build up my power or my fortune, nor to conquer the least important of my appetites or my habits. I am born a worker, French, with hereditary syphilis or tuberculosis. The history of a life, whatever it may be, is a story of frustration. The coefficient of adversity of things is such that it takes years of patience to obtain the most trifling result. Moreover it is necessary "to obey nature in order to command her", that is to say, to insert my action in the mesh of determinism. Much more than appearing "to make himself", man seems "to be made" by climate and land, race and class, language, the history of the collectivity of which he is part, heredity, the particular circumstances of his childhood, acquired habits, the great and the little events of his life.' (*L'Être et le Néant*, p. 561.)

It is true that the being called free is one that can realize his projects, but the rejection of what is actual and the projection of what is possible is the very meaning of free action, and the resistances encountered are the condition of action which makes the difference between liberty and necessity. 'There cannot be a free *pour-soi* save as engaged in a resistant world.' To be free does not mean practicability of purpose; it means determining what one wants, not getting what one wants, but determining what one wants in the large sense of choosing how one shall take one's life and what ends one shall pursue. At the same time, the autonomous choice is not a mere wish or aspiration, it is not real unless it initiates action: in this sense, the prisoner is always free to try to escape or to try to get himself liberated—as distinct from being free to walk out or to dream of being set free. Liberty is not in question until consciousness separates itself from the given, which is the foundation of knowledge and action, already a movement towards a new state of things. 'Thus liberty is lack of being in relation to a given being and not the emergence of a positive being.' It presupposes all being and cannot therefore be its own source. The facticity of liberty is its attachment to the given by separation from which it comes into existence. My place, my body, my past, my fundamental relation to the other person: these are the structural aspects of my total situation illumined by my projects.

My limitation of place is one of the forms of my facticity, but what that place means and whether it is an obstacle, an opportunity, a starting-point, a matter of indifference, depends upon my free projects. The past is determined irremediably, but its evaluation remains in suspense—what it means to me, what I make of it, the part it plays in my life. In a thousand ways, I can choose my past or repudiate it. What the sequel will be that is the key to the past is in the open future. Thus the Greeks would always say: Call no man happy until his death. The past does not determine the future. Rather, one must say: If you want to have such a past, act in such a way. I can choose and continue a tradition, repudiate or fulfil an engagement, learn from my experience or ignore it, overcome a proved weakness or avoid or exploit it; and in such ways I act freely on my past and convert it into motives by my choice of the future.

It is I who give meaning to my surroundings by my projects, and to the events which affect my projects: I create my situation and am responsible for it, and it is in this situation that I am free. When I separate myself in consciousness from what is there, I constitute not the world but its existence and meaning for me: it is by the independence and indifference of things and my capacity to separate myself from them and to act on them in order to change them for the sake of some project, a future end, that I have the liberty which I am. Purpose would be inconceivable save in an order of independent indifferent things, partly knowable, partly stable, partly alterable; and the practicability of purpose is conditioned in this way. Therefore intelligent purpose is open, empirical, modifiable. It is not that I simply interpret the world by my projects, and thus give things their coefficient of adversity or utility; it is that I form my projects partly on my experience of the use and potentiality of things, and allow for the unforeseeable.

This treatment of the world from the point of view of my interests and projects is complicated by the presence of others in the world. Not mainly because they enjoy a different perspective and form a different interpretation, but because most things are presented to me as already worked over, utilized, standardized for prescribed uses: instead of my giving them meaning by my projects, they tell me what to do, and therefore, since I am my projects, what I am; and since these ready-made meanings and public instructions of an already inhabited and organized world are not addressed to me personally but to everyone concerned, I am reduced to impersonality in adopting or obeying them. This world of defined meanings, available techniques, given ends, and other persons, is a matter of contingent fact, which cannot be deduced from the existence of the *pour-soi* itself in face of the *en-soi* as independent reality. It is by these means that I *live* my participation in the human species, as I live my body and my place. It is not I who decide by my projects whether I shall see the world in the simple clear-cut black and white of the proletarian or in the chiaroscuro of the bourgeois: 'I am not only thrown in front of brute existents, I am thrown into a working-class world, French, lorraine or méridional, which offers me its meanings without my having done anything to uncover them'. But these techniques and standardized meanings and instructions are not self-acting; they are techniques only when they are viewed from outside and analysed as used; in use they are spontaneous projections towards personal ends. Language is the cardinal example, furnished as it is by the elaboration of usage and formulable in grammatical rules, but in spontaneous use the phrase transcends the individual words and the thing denoted in a vivid personal intention; and this is only possible on the basis of established usage regulated by rule. The human world, worked over, standardized, furnished with instructions and techniques, conditions and facilitates liberty and does not replace it. It is in order to be a man that one belongs to a nation, a class, a family, etc.: these are the conditions of one's projects, which one both maintains and surpasses. It is from *these* conditions that I separate myself in my projects. And it is in this way that by my projects I help to make the human species itself, as language is made not by laws but by use.

Although the ready-made meanings and techniques furnished by others merely condition my liberty and do not limit it, the existence of others does limit my liberty. This is not merely that I cannot change and cannot even properly know the image or opinion which another may entertain of me; that would not matter: what is a fundamental objective fact of my being, which therefore can and does limit my liberty, is that from the moment when a liberty other than mine rises in face of me I begin to exist in a new dimension of being and, this time, there is no question of my conferring a meaning on brute existents, nor of turning to my own account the meaning which others have given to certain objects: it is I who see myself given a meaning, and it is not a meaning which I can get hold of or make use of. Here is a dimension of me which I cannot get rid of and cannot live; it is given and has to be endured. At this point and in this sense, I am something that I have not chosen to be. This limitation of my liberty is not at all the limitation imposed by others by means of prohibitions, but lies simply and solely in the mere fact that I am an object to another, and in that my lived situation (wholly informed by my liberty) becomes an objective structure: my being a Jew or a worker is not for another the lived situation it is for me, but is a determination. I can only recognize the liberty of another by accepting that; my outside which I cannot choose, nor know, nor adopt, is the liberty of others and the check or limit to my own. What I am in its absolute concreteness appears only to another; the words by which he describes it are abstract and I cannot apply them to myself. My characteristics are given, objective, for another who is not identified with them, and I who am identified with them cannot realize them: in this sense, my characteristics are unrealizable. They can be recognized to be unrealizable only when I try to realize them, which I do when I accept the other as free subject and myself as object for him. I do not receive passively the labels fixed on me— ugly, weak, Jew, etc.—I react to them according to my own fundamental projects, am proud, ashamed, indifferent, etc. Thus for others these characteristics simply *are*; for me they can only be as if chosen. I can neither refuse to be what I am for another nor simply be that: I have to digest it. These unrealizables, then (my characteristics in the eyes of another), are not brought into existence by me and constitute the limit and outside of my situation, yet they demand that I shall take them into account in terms of my fundamental project and in recognizing the free existence of the other. In this they resemble and share the nature of an imperative, which comes from outside and demands to be taken up in liberty and adopted as one's own, and yet can never lose its exteriority. Such is the unrealizable which demands to be realized. I cannot escape being the object of another's free existence, which limits my liberty, and I cannot live the situation and characteristics attributed to me by the other, but I can at least will this entire situation, to be limited by the freedom of the other; and this brings the external limit inside my situation, under my choice. I see that there is a liberty beyond my liberty, a situation beyond my situation, and that this involves my being there in the middle of the world for someone else, and by willing that situation and reacting to it in the circumstances of my particular case I bring it into my situation under my liberty, although it remains unrealizable. I cannot go outside and see myself as Frenchman or worker, but I can take it upon myself to be in order to be Frenchman or worker decisively. This is an alienation of myself: for myself, I *am* nothing.

Nor should the limit imposed by death be misconceived. Contrary to the conception of Heidegger that death is my sovereign possibility, death is not *my* possibility at all, it is 'a cancellation always possible of what I can be, which is outside my possibilities'. Death is accidental in its occurrence and therefore absurd: far from giving a life its meaning, it may leave that meaning in doubt and suspense. 'My project towards *a* death is comprehensible (as suicide, martyr, hero), but not the project towards *my* death as the indeterminate possibility of no longer realizing presence in the world, for this project would be the destruction of all projects. Thus death cannot be my peculiar possibility; it cannot even be one of *my* possibilities.' On the positive side, my death is the triumph of the point of view of the other over the point of view which I am: my whole life then simply *is*, and is no longer its own suspense, can no longer be changed by the mere consciousness which it has of itself. Life decides its own meaning because it is always in suspense; the life that is dead does not cease also to change, but the die is cast, it is what the living make of the dead and their works that is in question. The fate of the dead is always in the hands of the living. Death is not annihilation, but the lapse of my subjectivity out of the world; I leave behind meanings and traces which are my meanings and traces and which are modified at the hands of others: I exist solely in my dimension of exteriority. Therefore, to meditate on my life considering it from the standpoint of death would be to meditate on my subjectivity taking the point of view of another upon it, and that is impossible. Thus, contrary to Heidegger, death so far from being my own possibility is a contingent fact which as such escapes me in principle and belongs in its origin to my facticity. Death is a pure fact, like birth. I am not 'free in order to die' (Heidegger), but a free being who dies. I choose to assume my death as the inconceivable limit of my subjectivity, as I choose to be liberty limited by the fact of the liberty of another. In neither case do I encounter this limit as a fetter upon my liberty.

This, then, in sum is Sartre's account of human freedom. The *pour-soi* is nothing other than its situation; being-in-a-situation defines human presence in the world, in taking account at the same time of its being-there and of its being-beyond. Human presence in the world is, indeed, the being that is always beyond its being-there. And the situation is the organized totality of being-there interpreted and lived in and by being-beyond.

'It is this steep and dusty road, this burning thirst which I have, this refusal of people to give me a drink, because I have no money or I am not of their country or of their race; it is my abandonment in the midst of these hostile peoples, with this bodily fatigue which will perhaps prevent my attaining the end which I had fixed for myself. But it is also precisely this *end*, not in so far as I formulate it clearly and explicitly, but inasmuch as it is there, everywhere about me, as that which unifies and explains all these facts, that which organizes them in a whole which can be described instead of making of them a disordered nightmare.' (*L'Être et le Néant*, p. 634.)

The chosen end which illumines the given does so because it is chosen as transcending *this* given—ideals are concrete and empirical. The *pour-soi* does not emerge with an end already given in relation to the situation; but in 'making' the situation, it 'makes itself', and inversely.

This freedom involves responsibility. To be in a situation, which is the being of human presence in the world, is to be responsible for one's manner of being without being the origin of one's own being. I am inescapably responsible because my ends which are mine alone determine my situation. It is lived, not suffered; I am conscious of being the incontestable author of my life in the sense of what happens to me. I am responsible even for the wars that happen in my time.

'Thus, totally free, indistinguishable from the epoch of which I have chosen to be the meaning, as profoundly responsible for the war as if I had myself declared it, unable to live anything without integrating it into *my* situation, engaging myself wholly in it and marking it with my seal, I must have no remorse nor regrets as I have no excuse, for, from the moment of my emergence into being, I carry the weight of the world on my own, without anything or anybody being able to lighten the burden . . . .

'On these conditions, since every event in the world can disclose itself to me only as *opportunity* (opportunity taken advantage of, lost, neglected, etc.), or, better still, since everything that happens to us can be considered as a *chance*, that is to say, can appear to us only as a means of realizing this being which is in question in our being, and since others, as transcendences-transcended, are themselves also only *opportunities* and *chances*, the responsibility of the *pour-soi* extends to the whole world as a peopled-world. It is just for this reason that the *pour-soi* apprehends itself in dread, that is to say, as a being who is not the originator of his own being, nor of the being of the other, nor of the *en-soi* which form the world, but who is forced to decide on the meaning of being, in himself and everywhere outside of himself. He who realizes in dread his condition of being thrown into a responsibility which goes back even to his finding himself in the world, no longer has remorse, nor regret, nor excuse; he is no more than a liberty which is itself perfectly revealed and whose being lies in this very revelation. But . . . most of the time we take refuge from dread in self-deception.' Ibid., (pp. 641, 642.)

VIII

Since it is by the ends which he projects that the *pour-soi* is defined, it is essential to study such ends as the clue to human activity. The analysis by psychologists of human propensities is no help because it falsifies the character of human presence in the world to treat it as a substance having these attributes as desires, and desires are concrete forms of consciousness (desire of something), transcendent, projective; and the whole person is present in each form of behaviour (were it a gesture), which reveals the fundamental project which is the person. What is this project? The *pour-soi* is the refusal to be the *en-soi* it comes into being by separating itself from, and is itself a project to be. What? The *pour-soi* comes into being as not the *en-soi* and this negation defines itself as projection towards the *en-soi*: between the *en-soi* denied and the *en-soi* projected, the *pour-soi* is nothing. The end and the aim of this negation that I am is the *en-soi*. Human presence in the world is the desire to be *en-soi*. But of course not the *en-soi* already encountered and rejected. The rejection is itself tantamount to a revolt of the *en-soi* against its own contingency, its gratuitousness, its absurdity. To say that the *pour-soi* lives its facticity is to say that this rejection is a vain effort of a being to found its own being. The being the *pour-soi* aspires to be is an *en-soi* that would be its own source, that is, which would be to its facticity as the *pour-soi* is to its motivations. It is consciousness identified with what it is conscious of without the least separation that the *pour-soi* desires to be, consciousness which would be founder of its own being in itself by the pure consciousness which it would have of itself. That is the ideal of God. Man is fundamentally desire to be God. This is the ultimate meaning of human desires and ends but does not constitute them what they are in their particularity, which is free invention. The desire to be which is ultimately desire to be founder of my own being is in practice desire expressed in choice of manner of being, what I do with my facticity.

'Thus we are faced with symbolic structures of great complexity which have *at least* three levels. In the empirical desire, I can discern a symbolization of the fundamental and concrete desire which is *the person* and which represents the way in which he has decided that being shall be in question in his being; and this fundamental desire, in its turn, expresses concretely and in the world, in the particular situation which surrounds the person, an abstract and significant structure which is the desire of being in general and which must be considered as *human reality in the person*, that which makes his community with another, that which makes it possible to affirm that there is a truth concerning man and not merely incomparable individuals.

138

. . . the desire of being, in its abstract purity, is the *truth* of the fundamental concrete desire, but does not exist in a real sense . . . the structure, abstract and ontological, "desire of being" could hardly represent the fundamental and *human* structure of the person, it could not be a fetter on his liberty. Liberty, indeed, is strictly assimilable to the cancellation of being: the only being which can be called free is the being which cancels (separates itself from) its being. We know, moreover, that the cancellation is *lack of being* and cannot be otherwise. Liberty is precisely being which makes itself lack of being. But since desire, as we have shown, is identical with lack of being, liberty can emerge only as being which makes itself desire of being, that is to say, as the project of the *pour-soi* to be *en-soi–pour-soi*. We have reached here an abstract structure which cannot at all be considered as the nature or essence of liberty, for liberty is existence and its existence precedes its essence; liberty is an emergence that is immediately concrete and is not distinguished from its choice, that is to say, from the *person*. But the structure under consideration may be called the *truth* of liberty, that is to say that it is the human meaning of liberty.' (Ibid., 654, 655.)

The ontological analysis once it has revealed the structure of man and the ultimate meaning of desire gives place to the empirical analysis of man's activities in the pursuit of the objects of his desire. Desire is at bottom the lack of being, a movement towards completion. Human presence in the world is a form of being separated from the *en-soi* which is wholly and solely what it is and by the mere fact of this separation striving for a consciousness which is not a consciousness of separation from but of identity with, a consciousness which founds itself, is its own cause. This desire is manifested in the abundant and diverse activities of men, seeking to do and to make, to have and to be. To trace in these varied activities prompted by human desire the forms of the fundamental human project to be a self-caused-thing-in-itself is the work of an existential psycho-analysis.

In the first place, the activity of doing and making can be reduced to a case of being or, far more usually, of having. In making something or creating a work of art, the artist is seeking to possess something outside himself which he encounters in the world and which bears the mark of himself; in seeking to know, the scientist seeks to appropriate the object known in a way that makes it his own and at the same time leaves it public and objective; in games and sports, the player seeks the appropriation of victory, not merely the prize but the difficulty overcome, mastery of the mountain, the sea, the air; and in the purest forms of play, it is not possession that is sought but being, realization in the purest form of the liberty of the person, the purest symbolization of the project to be God which is the profound meaning of human presence in the world. Thus these typical activities of human life reveal a striving to appropriate the *en-soi* in its absolute being, beyond the typical objects of appropriation which represent it. Human desire, then, in its practical activities is concentrated upon possession of the *en-soi* in various forms and by various means; in its ideal activity it is aiming at a form of being which unites the nature of *en-soi* and *pour-soi*. What is the relation between this practical appropriation of the *en-soi* and the form of being which is the ultimate aim?

The answer is that the desire to have, to possess, is a desire to be united with the object in a certain relation, that is, a desire for a certain form of being. The object possessed remains what it is, unaffected, external; but the possession of it by the *pour-soi* is the attempt to internalize it, to make it an extension and a part of the being of the *pour-soi*. *Mine* is a form of being intermediary between the absolute inwardness of me and the absolute externality of not-me. It aims at an ideal identity. The possessor becomes the *raison d'être* of the object possessed; and virtually I am the creator and user of the objects with which I surround myself and by which I live. It is only the act of creation or of use which realizes the ideal identity or union of person and thing; outside of this, the thing lapses into an indifferent object encountered. But the *pour-soi* because it is nothing in search of its being throws all the accent on the object possessed: I am identified with the thing as the completion of my being; in giving the thing its *raison d'être* and identifying myself with it, I am in some sense what I seek to be, *en-soi–pour-soi*. In possessing, I have outside myself in the world a form of myself which I can enjoy as an object; and in this I anticipate my being-for-another: I am already in possession, enjoying myself as an object from outside, which the other wants to make of me.

But this possession is merely a symbolic realization of the ideal human project and does not give satisfaction. It is for that reason that possession is insatiable and often passes into destruction, whether by using up or wearing out or by deliberate action. To destroy is akin to creation, in that it assimilates the object to the self, even more completely; and when it has gone it remains in the sense that there was this independent object which is now assimilated. To give away is similarly a form of destroying and of possessing.

What fundamentally is this relation of possessing? It is that I as *raison d'être* of the object seek to appropriate its being, and, beyond and through its being, the world itself; and since the object is itself in some sense ideally me in being mine, the *pour-soi* is here its own *raison d'être* existing in the mode of *en-soi*. 'To be in the world is to seek to possess the world, that is to say, to seize the total world as what is lacking to the *pour-soi* in order that it may become *en-soi-pour-soi*'. What is sought here is not an abstract mode of being but a concrete union. The *pour-soi* chooses this world in and by the concrete object, that-there, and transcends it towards a new state of the same world in which being will be *en-soi* founded by the *pour-soi*.

Thus the desire to have is indirectly the desire to be, both springing from the lack of being which I am. This nothing which I make myself to be in coming into existence as consciousness is itself individual and concrete, being the lack of the being which already exists and in the midst of which I arise. Thus I choose being in a thousand ways of being and having. The business of an existential psycho-analysis is to trace why I choose to possess the world by means of this or that particular object. That certainly belongs to liberty, but the objects themselves can be studied and made to reveal being in their qualities. 'For it is not at the level of taste for the sweet or the bitter, etc., that free choice is irreducible, but at the level of choice of the aspect of being which is revealed *through and by means of* the sweet, the bitter, etc.'

Human presence in the world, then, is fundamentally a choice of being, either directly or indirectly, through appropriation of the world by means of concrete things in the world. When the choice is by means of appropriation, each thing is chosen for the way in which it gives off being, the way in which being crops out at its surface. Thus there is wanted a psycho-analysis of things and of their matter which is concerned to establish the way in which each thing is an objective symbol of being and of the relation of human presence in the world to this being.

The quality of a thing is nothing other than its being, and not a mere subjective mode of apprehension; and the whole being is present in any quality: it is the disclosure of being to a consciousness, which separates itself from being so that there is being for something which is not that being. It is this separation, making it that there is being disclosed in its qualities, that the *pour-soi* desires to overcome in order to reach being such as it is absolutely and in itself. 'In each apprehension of quality, there is, in this sense, a metaphysical effort to escape from our condition, in order to pierce the muff of nothingness of the *there is* (of consciousness) and penetrate to the pure *en-soi*.' But obviously we can only seize the quality as symbol of a being which escapes us totally although it is totally there in front of us. Nevertheless, this attempt to get an intuition of being by means of the qualities disclosed in things can be helped and illumined by a psycho-analysis of the symbolism of things. The yellow, the rough, the polished; water and oil; the fluid and solid; the animal: here are forms of being which have their meanings which throw light on the human choice of being in its particular manifestations. When I separate myself from something (which is my consciousness of it) I do not merely hold off it in awareness of it, I ask implicitly, How can I be it? How can I have it? Its response is in its materiality, the way it gives itself; its nature is its response to this question of appropriation. Thus, the viscous gives itself readily, but when it is taken it adheres: it symbolizes, not the domination of the *pour-soi* over the *en-soi* which it founds and uses, but an ideal form of being in which the psychic and the physical are confused, and the *pour-soi* is sucked into and possessed by the *en-soi*. This ideal of being can no more be realized than the union in which both elements retain their distinctiveness; but it remains a danger, an anti-value, as the other remains an end, the supreme value. Thus there are no tastes however seemingly idle and indifferent which do not throw light on our fundamental project and the way in which we go about to realize it.

'Each human presence in the world is at the same time the direct project of metamorphosing his own *Pour-soi* into *En-soi–Pour-soi* and the project of appropriating the world as the totality of being-in-itself, under the varieties of a fundamental quality. Every human presence in the world is a passion, in that it is a project to lose itself in order to found being and in the same act constitute the *En-soi* which escapes contingency in being its own ground, the *Ens causa sui* which the religions call God. Thus man's passion is the inverse of Christ's, for man loses himself as man in order that God may be born. But the idea of God is contradictory and we lose ourselves in vain; man is a useless passion.' (Ibid., 708.)

IX

The foregoing summary of the argument does no justice at all to the intellectual rigour, ingenuity, and copious description of Sartre's own exposition throughout more than 700 pages of *L'Être et le Néant*. His account of human presence in the world is likely to be rejected by common sense as bizarre, perverse, bewildering, and depressing, throwing no light on human problems and helping nobody to live more intelligently or effectively. Philosophers of course have their own sophisticated way of dealing with it. Sartre is far too intelligent a thinker to be easily vulnerable to common sense, and too well versed in philosophy not to have anticipated objections from the orthodox standpoints. The hail of obvious and superficial criticism is not likely to inflict any vital wound. Of course he is open to serious criticism—on the condition that he is taken seriously.

The point that his philosophy is pessimistic and depressing is easily disposed of. In order to know how to live and to live well, it is first necessary to know on what conditions we have to live; diagnosis comes before prescription. Both Sartre himself and Simone de Beauvoir have made this clear, and have acutely pointed out that the pessimism and cynicism of popular wisdom show that people have no objection to such views of human nature and destiny, as they have none to sentimental and romantic views; what they do object to is the view that is disturbing: they want to think that to live well is easy or is impossible, not to be told that it is both difficult and possible.

But is the diagnosis right? What is gained by refurbishing such metaphysical entities as the *en-soi* and the *pour-soi* instead of relying wholly upon the empirical descriptions and conceptions of the sciences, especially psychology, to give the account of nature and man and human life in the world? Sartre insists that empirical psychology is not based on anything ultimate at all, since it is either concerned first and last with facts or relies for its explanations on the libido, the will to power, a bundle of original propensities, the mechanism of the association of ideas, that is to say, on some empirical finding or uncriticized assumption or metaphysical entity. It does not go back to any evident original principle which can really be the source of explanation. Hegel had complained of modern philosophy that it stultified itself by founding metaphysics on psychological facts which themselves required to be explained, and Husserl, taking the task of philosophy seriously, explored the meaning of meaning by trying to uncover the ultimate structures of consciousness. Sartre claims that his ontology gives the mental and moral sciences their principles, and he himself has made extensive application of his own doctrine in sustained psychological and social analysis, abstract and concrete, not without striking results. His studies of Baudelaire and of anti-semitism, and his theory of the emotions and of the imagination, are remarkably fruitful, and fruitful because of his doctrinal approach, whether or not he really succeeds in laying bare his ontology in the complex structures of the phenomena he studies.

Before raising the question of its truth, the boldness and the philosophical virtues of Sartre's doctrine are worth a word of appreciation. With beautiful economy, consciousness (simply by making itself other than the world without being something other than the world) constitutes the world and the self and the principle of all knowing, feeling, and striving, without a trace of traditional idealism or materialism. (Marcel describes this as obsolete idealism united with old-fashioned materialism, in an essay on Sartre which is certainly not lacking in truth save in the total omission of all that is positive in the man and in the philosophy.) This enables Sartre to give us both a palpable natural world (with a reconditioned fascinated interest in the simple materiality of things) and human presence in the world as liberty—conditions of the carnal, spiritual, and dramatic satisfactions of human living. Consciousness by its very lack of being is choice of being, and from that original project which consciousness is springs all the diversity of human activity, even the ontology which analyses and conceptualizes the original project, and thus modifies my own sidelong awareness of my consciousness, that is, this original project itself which I live and am. The rational ideal of philosophy is here approached to the point where further progress is fatally balked. The explanatory description reaches its limit with the conditions that give us a world, and the rational end which it discloses as the ideal goal of human striving is seen to be unattainable. Human existence is presented as the historical attempt to realize the union of consciousness and existence (*En-soi–Pour-soi*), as classical philosophy has been the attempt to deduce existence from thought in order to see the world as rationally necessary. This project, unachieved in philosophy because the world is not required by reason, will not be achieved in history because the world cannot be made wholly rational, even if philosophy turns from explaining to changing it. The ideal is and remains self-contradictory; nevertheless, it is and remains the explanation of human activity, even if recognition of the contradiction modifies human aspiration and effort. What makes Sartre's argument fascinating philosophically is the ingenuity with which he makes the simple presence of consciousness to the given material world suffice in its manner to account for everything in heaven and earth, clarifying not only human life in the world but also past efforts in philosophy, and seeming neatly to avoid the difficulties and save the values of opposed schools. No doubt his triumph is a Pyrrhic victory, not merely because the cost of it is an insurmountable discrepancy between the ideal and the actual, but mainly because the argument raises theoretical difficulties not less stubborn than those which it evades or resolves: my consciousness of something and implicit awareness of this consciousness, which is the foundation of all, is not awareness of me and can never reach me; the *pour-soi* as pure flight and pursuit can never know itself as flight and pursuit, and therefore the principle which ingeniously furnishes the ontological description from within could never produce the reflective consciousness which carries out the description. But, leaving aside technical soundness in this general consideration of Sartre's philosophy, the prior question is whether this type of analysis really is explanatory. Is there necessarily an ultimate irreducible situation in terms of which human life is bound to be lived, so that every human activity can be interpreted through intermediary structures in terms of this absolute situation? Or is this an entirely otiose reductive analysis, even less excusable than reductive materialism?

We have become used in Freudian psychology to the idea of fantastic infantile wishes, incapable of being realized and normally repressed and lost, which play their part in the development of mature desires; but Sartre's primordial structure is the very being of human presence in the world and conditions all empirical desires and therefore cannot play the part of a mere component. Its status is unique, and is not to be confused with that of material structures in mechanical determinism or of psychic structures in psychological determinism. It is not a 'fetter on liberty', it is 'the human meaning of liberty'. No primitive structure continues to limit the meaning and possibilities of later elaborations—to suppose that it does is the reductive fallacy. Sartre, however, gives a dazzling performance on the ice that will bear nobody else; he escapes the fallacy and exploits its power of reductive explanation. He does it with inventive resourcefulness in the one way possible, by keeping consciousness clear of the complications and elaborations of being, consciousness remains first and last detached non-being and at the same time constitutive of all we know and are: it is the play of light, revealing the world, inseparable from the world, and never mixed or compounded or entering into process with anything in the world. And he can use this principle of explanation not in the manner of traditional determinism, whether causal or final, but as omnipresent and constitutive, which acquits him of relying on exploded forms of rationalism. His daring and simple conception, with the elaborate and impressive manner of its working out in the full knowledge of what he is about, makes, at worst, one more monumental failure of the speculative genius of man. But the intellectual ingenuity addressed to the traditional problems of technical philosophy is rooted in the total responses of the man, and is not a *tour de force*. Sartre's famous nausea, his sense and horror of the gratuitousness of things, cognate with his repugnance to the viscous and the animal and his preference for the metallic and quasi-metallic, indicate a profound rationalism as the crying need of his nature, and the lived impulse of his philosophy; but it is a rationalism that learns to abandon the quest for origins and ends and to rejoice in an absolute 'without cause, without reason, without goal, without any past or future other than its own permanence, gratuitous, fortuitous, magnificent'. (*Le Sursis*, p. 276.) Consciousness as the play of light on the surface of things is man's glory and his agony, since it is his being; and there is no doubt that Sartre lives it as such.

Sartre is a rationalist and a materialist, as Marcel says he is; but there is no sense in dismissing him under these labels as no different from old-fashioned gentlemen of this description whom one may have learned to despise—or perhaps to fear. There have always been rationalists and materialists as long as man has been reflective enough for these terms to have any meaning, and there always will be as long as the same condition holds. The point about Sartre's rationalism and materialism is that it is an original attempt of a highly vital and gifted living person to get a grip on his own experience and come to terms with life. As such it is profoundly interesting and instructive to anybody who is not too antipathetic to profit by it.

If he is a rationalist and materialist, how is it possible to include Sartre in the existentialist camp? Indeed, Marcel would exclude him on the ground that he is a rationalist, or else an eccentric. The answer is that Sartre is not a rationalist or materialist of any previous type. His filiation from Heidegger and Husserl shows his tendency, and his language and choice and treatment of themes confirm it. His whole philosophy is constructed (whether soundly or not) on the lived project which consciousness is. Man is resolved into his situation, into his relations and projects, not into any essence or nature. Man is in absolute ethical isolation and totally responsible. These exemplify the theses of existentialism, not those of rationalism or of materialism.

Finally, the destructiveness or nihilism of Sartre's philosophy calls for remark. He concludes the argument of *L'Être et le Néant* with the words, 'man is a useless passion'. Simone de Beauvoir, speaking for Sartre, in the first chapter of her *Pour une Morale de l'Ambiguïté* takes up the point. True, there is this frustration in the pursuit of his ideal, but it is the condition of man's existence by which he becomes present to the world: he is for ever prevented from being the world, but it is by this separation that the world *is* for him. His despair and his delight are two sides of one medal. Man comes into existence for himself and brings the world into existence for himself by the ceaseless separation and projection of himself. That is his destiny, and nothing can save man from himself. Instead of hiding from himself or looking for salvation from himself, which he can only gain at the price of his abolition, man must come to himself and take his destiny upon himself. This is the conversion of which Sartre speaks, which leads to salvation of the whole man by the whole man achieved on this earth. The converted man, who is awakened to his human condition and has assumed it, plunges into the world but does not lose himself in the world: he accepts total responsibility and engages himself fully, and always maintains the separation from himself which constitutes his actions personal, so that they have value and give value. 'The business of any morality is to consider human life as a match which can be won or lost, and to teach men how to win.' But it is up to men individually to choose their ends and their values, and thus to constitute for themselves the meaning of success and failure. The risks are real and the frustrations inevitable; but life is lived by taking the risks and fighting ceaselessly against frustration. Consciousness whose being it is not to be the being to which it is present serves in the pages of *L'Être et le Néant* as the principle of explanation of the natural order of human existence in the world. When the person makes himself lack of being, he understands that he is both *pour-soi* and *en-soi* and that he can never satisfactorily suppress either nor unite both: at the same time, he enters upon the distinctively human life and tackles the problem with a passion that is not useless. The natural order of this human existence is willed and becomes a moral order; he is no longer explained, he is justified: he justifies himself.

The nihilism of the modern age had undermined everything, working on every front in the guise of a humanism that had given up thinking about ultimate questions. Sartre proposes to clear the ruins and reconstruct a dogmatic humanism which understands and assumes the eternal human situation, offering a liberation of mankind which starts with a total knowledge of man by himself.

VII

A PHILOSOPHY OF PERSONAL EXISTENCE

'PHILOSOPHY', remarks Schopenhauer, 'like the overture to *Don Juan*, begins with a minor chord.' For it is astonished, meditative, measured preoccupation with the problem of existence perceived in its magnitude: its possible impossibility, Heidegger says; the preferability of non-existence, Schopenhauer says. Antoine Roquentin, hero of Sartre's first novel *La Nausée*, has no great expectations and therefore does not fall into disillusionment and despair, but he is stunned with astonishment at this life which he finds that he has—for no reason, for nothing: there is the oppressive tumid presence of vegetation that spreads itself out excessively, offensively, stupidly, manifesting the amorphous material paste of things without rational subordination to the functions it covers; and there is the face of these same things (the chestnut tree, the laurels) smiling as though wanting to say something, seeming like thoughts which had stopped short and lapsed into oblivion and yet retained a queer vestigial quiver of meaning for ever out of reach. What is man to make of this Being which envelops him, and which he is? So many attitudes and interpretations are possible. Schopenhauer condemns and refuses Being as evil. Classical philosophy attempts to rationalize and to think Being. The many forms of scepticism and agnosticism agree in finding no possibility of certainty in answer to the question of Being. Existentialism also is a philosophy of Being, a philosophy

149

of attestation and acceptance, and a refusal of the attempt to rational-ize and to think Being. Being can be experienced in a personal venture to which philosophy is the call. Yet the themes of refusal and agnosticism and rationalism are also heard in this new composition. We are given a world whose pretensions must be broken, a world to be both accepted and refused, a life to be built on the further side of despair; knowledge being irremediably incomplete and uncertain throws the weight of responsibility upon personal decision; reason alone can limit reason, and its present duty is to restore the concrete and thus to eliminate the false theoretical problems which have haunted philosophy and illumine the real problems for which there are no theoretical solutions. As each aspect of the human situation is lit up, the light is reflected upon the personal isolation and re-sponsibility of the existing individual at the centre.

Philosophy begins as an interruption, a hold-up which puts all in question, a suspense of spontaneity and normality: it is a separation of mind and body, of the citizen and his city, of man and the world. The problem is to get things going again, by justifying them with reasons; the questions must be answered, the universality and neces-sity of things assured. For Hegel, haunted by the ideal Republic of Plato and by the real city of classical times (in which each had his place and his part and enjoyed expansion and self-transcendence by participation in a system of absolute good), the separation happened in history and was perfected in and by Judaism and Christianity; but it is repeated in the individual consciousness, for I know myself by what I have become, in my destiny, and yet I am other than that and have to reconcile myself with my destiny and take it upon me—'destiny is the consciousness of oneself but as of an enemy'. The reconciliation like the separation takes place in history, when the individual finds in the institutions, activities, and destiny of his people a concrete universal life akin to his own and appealing to it with which to incorporate himself. This identification of the indivi-dual with the world through his people restores the concrete life of the spirit, for world history is itself the objectification of the Absolute—just as I know myself by what I have become. For Hegel, then, the separation of man and the world which is the occasion of philosophy can be healed because the ideal and the actual are reconciled in the life of a people which is a concrete universal to which the life of the individual can be assimilated and in which it is consummated; and he criticized Kant and Fichte with whose thought (as with Schlegel's) he was closely concerned because they made the ideal and the actual irreconcilable in putting the separation between reason as the law of man's being and the natural world of empirical selves which it must rule and could never subdue. For existentialists, the separation is the foundation of all foundations, and to abolish it in a total reconciliation is to undermine personal existence itself. Existentialists cannot accept the concrete universal of Hegel as a solution for two reasons: (1) history is the quantitative factual outcome of the individual decisions of others and can have no authority for the existing individual unless he chooses to give it such; (2) knowledge can only be partial knowledge of the past; the future remains open, 'man is the future of man'. They cannot accept the abstract universal of Kant, even in the practical form which Fichte gave it, as a solution because man has no essence whose right and destiny it is to rule and engross all. Man is only what he does, yet is always beyond what he does, without being anything in substance or in essence within himself: he confronts his empirical self and his historical existence in the actual world, and becomes human by what he makes his own and what he repudiates and what he projects—although of course he more commonly hides from himself in the labyrinthine forms of inauthenticity. There is no profounder self in the depths of the personality, a soul of good within to which man seldom or never does justice; it is simply that he is always in question, always beyond himself, always infinitely more than what he would be if he were reduced to being what he is, that in good and in evil he is beyond himself always, and this separation is the principle of personal existence. In Sartre's play *Huis Clos*, at the outset on his arrival in hell, Garcin sees that it is life without a break: the eyelids are fixed and don't blink, no eye-blink and no sleep. The eye-blink ('four thousand little rests per hour') is symbolic of perpetual self-renewal, with its regular exits and impromptu returns, which is the structure of human presence in the world. The moral of the play is not the cry of Garcin towards the end, 'Hell is . . . other people!' It is the horror of human consciousness if it could not break off, if it could not be new, if it could only go on reproducing the past, if it were really determined, a fate.

The peculiarity of existentialism, then, is that it deals with the separation of man from himself and from the world, which raises the questions of philosophy, not by attempting to establish some universal form of justification which will enable man to readjust himself but by permanently enlarging and lining the separation itself as primordial and constitutive for personal existence. The main business of this philosophy therefore is not to answer the questions which are raised but to drive home the questions themselves until they engage the whole man and are made personal, urgent, and anguished. Such questions cannot be merely the traditional questions of the schools nor merely disinterested questions of curiosity concerning the conditions of knowledge or of moral or aesthetic judgements, for what is put in question by the separation of man from himself and from the world is his own being and the being of the objective world. In this sense, existentialism goes back to the beginning of philosophy and appeals to all men to awaken from their dogmatic slumbers and discover what it means to become a human being. But if man is a suspense of being, always in question, and if the objective world is also permanently in question because of the irremovable ambiguity of nature and of history and the enigmatic silence of the cosmos, what is the use of a philosophy which instigates and insists on questions that have no possibility of an answer?

These questions are not theoretical but existential, the scission which makes the existing individual aware of himself and of the world in which he is makes him a question to himself and life a question to him. They are questions which can be blurred or dodged, and they normally are; and therefore it is the first business of philosophy to enlarge them until they engross the whole man. The reason why there can be no objective, universal, and certain answer to them is not merely the present inadequacy of our knowledge but because man is and remains in his being a question, a personal choice, and the objective world is and remains in its being a question, open possibility: both are at any time other than and more than anything that can be said of them. Being is, in Marcel's language, not a problem to be mastered and done with but a mystery to be lived and re-lived. But the being of man and of the world is not wholly and solely a question, the question is a penumbra which persists around a dense circle of actual choice and first-hand experience. The second business of philosophy, then, is to cure the mind of looking for illusory objective universal answers, and to aid the person in making himself and getting his experience. If, as Marcel says, the first question is whether I shall live or not, whether to take on this life which I find I have for no reason, whether to assume this destiny which I am and try to inform with will and reason this merely natural and fortuitous empirical self, it is a question for me alone and it would be absurd to look for an objective answer: there can be no answer that is not my own personally responsible decision. Of course I cannot reasonably make up my mind until I know what I am in for, and it may seem reasonable to ask for the information on which to take a decision: what is this human life I am invited to live? Existential philosophies insist that any plain and positive answer is false, because the truth is in the insurmountable ambiguity which is at the heart of man and of the world. In Jaspers and Marcel it is plainly the ambiguity of a world which invites despair and instigates faith, without any possibility of objective certainty that would remove the risks. But in Nietzsche and Sartre, who reject philosophic and religious faith, the ambiguity remains, the ambivalence of values, the ambiguity of man who is both a thing and not a thing. Sartre gives the most dogmatic answer, but it is only an elaboration of this ambiguity which man introduces into the world in being what he is and of the impossibility of overcoming it: he seems to be giving the positive answer that human life is man's vain attempt to overcome his separation and adjust himself perfectly to the world, but this is not a verdict, for it is the ideal aspect of the fact that neither a man nor the world is just what can be said of them—the adjustment is practical, partial, and continuous. The quest for certainty is bound up with the conception of a ready-made universe of which I can make a theoretical model, a rational system in which I have an appointed place and part. Hegel's was the last monumental attempt of philosophy to think Being in this way. But if existence cannot be thought, if I am an intelligence immersed in a larger reality which is not a closed intelligible system, if knowledge as such is a type of perspective, and any given knowledge a perspective within a perspective, I reach the object not by exhaustive knowledge of its laws in constant contexts but by inexhaustible experience of its concreteness in varied contexts; and therefore the past has no final authority over the future, universals are informative but not binding, and if I heal my separation from the world by identifying myself with it wholly and finally in any shape or form I extinguish my own being and the being of the world for me.

Therefore existential philosophies are concerned with the manoeuvre of existing individuals whose being is ambiguous (both bound and free, separated and joined) in a total existence which is ambiguous (finite and infinite, end and means, a plenitude and nothing).

The manoeuvre consists not merely in preventing one side of the ambiguity from destroying the other, but in using each to reinforce the other. Existence lies beyond thought, and beyond existence is possibly some form of transcendence: this is the field of personal venture and experience in which the manoeuvre takes place. The business of existential philosophy in helping the person to make himself and get his experience is to furnish analyses of the concrete structures of first-hand experience in which the ambiguities are operative: certain affective states (nausea, ennui, dread, joy) which reveal Being by wiping away the familiar face of things and dissolving subjective pre-conceptions; the presence in fidelity of one person to another in their pure subjectivity in which each is other than what he is known to be—or the structural impossibility of this presence; the tension of being and having in sport and artistic creation; the bounded situations which have to be lived in faith or despair. As Marcel puts it, the typical philosophies (materialism, idealism, theology) in their typical forms abolish ideally the separation of man and the world, and thereby destroy his being which lies in living the tension of the ideal and the actual. As Jaspers says, in effect, since Being cannot be domesticated nor administered and there is no truth about Being which can be formulated and distributed, there is a sense in which all philosophies are true and all are false: false as undertaking to tell the truth about Being, whether negative or positive; true as inviting or throwing one into some type of experience. Since thought cannot think existence, its business is to initiate and interpret experience. Its tentatives in this kind may be dubious or even arbitrary, but at least it is always being put in question and put to the test and does not congeal into a substitute for experience. It is in objective certainty and established knowledge that Heidegger, like Kierkegaard, sees the grave of truth.

Existentialists are commonly ridiculed for dramatizing the ordinary. Sensible people accept the contingency of the world and get on with the job of living in it. Existentialists moan in anguish to find themselves gratuitous and derelict in a possibly impossible world, shelterless orphans deprived of the mother comfort of reason and necessity. Everybody solemnly quotes the saying of Plato that to be astonished is the truly philosophical feeling. What else but a first-hand recovery of wonder is this nausea and all its related affects? Plato's philosophical wonder is excited by the vision of an intelligible system of Being, a rational harmony repeated in the virtuous man, the ideal republic, and the organic cosmos. The philosophical wonder inaugurated by nausea is excited by the sense of a different type of order. The discovery of the world as gratuitous and absurd (its acceptance as given, in unemotional words) is not disillusionment, nor wild grief that God is dead, nor stoical resignation, nor anything of the sort; it is, above all, the context which brings out the meaning of man's separation from himself and from the world, which is the existential root of all philosophies and the foundation of all foundations in existential philosophies. If the speculative fantasies of the classical rationalist philosophies were true in principle, and the individual could be assigned an appointed place in a system, man as man would not exist. Man's separation is a malaise, but it is not nostalgia for the Great Chain of Being; it is a disorder which founds and refounds the human order of possibilities which are temporal and modest and never final. In this order, the existing individual has no refuge from continuous responsibility. But why the anguished responsibility of the existentialist? A certain anxiety in carrying out given tasks and duties, a fear of not being equal to the demands, is understandable enough; and normal people feel acute anxiety in the midst of the uncertainties which beset an original decision: but these are only echoes of the primordial anxiety felt by the man who knows that at every moment in absolute solitariness he is responsible for the fate of man. This absolute responsibility of the individual can be treated as a platitude, or it may be held to be the fundamental truth about the individual which he is most reluctant to face and accept although he is only authentically man in so far as he lives and acts in the full consciousness of it. When there is prevailing confidence in established values and authorities, the primordial, absolute and solitary responsibility of the individual is regarded either as a meaningless platitude or as a dangerous thought; in less settled times, it may come vividly home to some as a sharp and searching truth, and when they exhibit it dramatically they are not (as it has been said) beating their breasts in a vain and stupid lament that values are not objective in the same sense as scientific knowledge. They are acutely aware that only the solitariness of decision discharges the responsibility responsibly. The case of Sartre exemplifies this.

Marcel, with the most emphatic disapproval, quotes the following from Sartre. 'My freedom is the unique foundation of values. And since I am the being by virtue of whom values exist, nothing—

absolutely nothing—can justify me in adopting this or that value or scale of values. As the unique basis of the existence of values, I am totally unjustifiable. And my freedom is in anguish at finding that it is the baseless basis of values.' On humanist assumptions, values are human valuations; and the public values of a society or a civilization are contributed and upheld by private individual choice. Sartre puts the being of man in his not-being, his negative capability, his power and right to secede, and therefore the individual is not relieved of his responsibility to choose for himself all over again, and stands in primitive isolation even though he is bound in place by the demands and pressures of modern industrial society. This view of the relation of individual valuations to social valuations is an intellectual myth of our time, like the social contract of earlier generations, both true and false. Rationalism, emancipation, enlightenment, education for change, these are the progressive influences that have encouraged detachment and scepticism, freedom from ties and traditions as well as from prejudices and superstititions. Such is the modern evacuated condition of Orestes in *Les Mouches* and of Mathieu in *Les Chemins de la Liberté*. Sartre himself is in revolt (with reservations) against the values of bourgeois society. His revolt, however, is not an inverted acceptance, a fear of freedom, such as he supposes Baudelaire's to have been—the type of the rebel intellectual; it is a revolt which accepts and rejoices in and trembles under the burden of responsibility for a new order. Sartre makes total responsibility the obverse of the power to secede which man is: they belong together inseparably. This puts him with Nietzsche, makes him an existentialist and not, for example, a surrealist. But why not a Marxist, since it is precisely Marxism which attacks bourgeois society and proposes to replace it? Indeed, that is the capital question to ask about Sartre, for he fully accepts the Marxist analysis of capitalism. We know what the Marxist answer is, for Sartre and his school have been much engaged in controversy with communists in France; and there is the elaborate examination of existentialism by the Hungarian Marxist Professor Lukacs, who treats it as the last vain effort of bourgeois intellectuals to find a third way beyond materialism and a bankrupt idealism, an effort to remain in the metaphysical world of ideas and ideals in order to escape having to accept historical socialism as it exists in concrete reality in the Soviet Union—as eighteenth-century philosophers invented a conceptual Deism to make a third way between atheism and positive historical or mystical religion, and to oppose the Church. Sartre, indeed, does oppose metaphysics to history in putting the being of man in the power to secede, as a metaphysical absolute independent of historical conditions. In *L'Être et le Néant,* he condemns the spirit of literal seriousness which attributes greater reality to the world than to oneself, or attributes reality to oneself in so far as one belongs to the world. Seriousness in this sense, he says, is the abdication of human presence in favour of the world, and the serious person buries his consciousness of his liberty at the bottom of himself. He adds: 'Marx posed the chief dogma of seriousness when he affirmed the priority of the object over the subject, and man is serious when he takes himself for an object'. Dialectical materialism makes good and evil vanish conjointly, for it abolishes their source.

Sartre, therefore, cannot be a Marxist because Marx, like Hegel, missed the permanent meaning of man's separation from himself and from the world and Marxist theory deprives man of his real being. But Sartre's own actual secession and total responsibility involves him in political action, reinforced in theory and in practice by his experience of the Resistance Movement in France during the German occupation. In those extreme circumstances, the isolation of the existing individual, his original and solitary responsibility for the essence and the fate of man, was not merely a moral platitude nor a metaphysical idea, but was the visible personal presence of men.

'For political realism as for philosophical idealism Evil was not a very serious matter.

'We have been taught to take it seriously. It is neither our fault nor our merit if we lived in a time when torture was a daily fact. Châteaubriand, Oradour, the Rue des Saussaies, Dachau, and Auschwitz have all demonstrated to us that Evil is not an appearance, that knowing its cause does not dispel it, that it is not opposed to Good as a confused idea is to a clear one, that it is not the effects of passions which might be cured, of a fear which might be overcome, of a passing aberration which might be excused, of an ignorance which might be enlightened, that it can in no way be diverted, brought back, reduced, and incorporated into idealistic humanism, like that shade of which Leibnitz has written that it is necessary for the glare of daylight. . . .

'Perhaps a day will come when a happy age, looking back at the past, will see in this suffering and shame one of the paths which led to peace. But we are not on the side of history already made. We were, as I have said, *situated* in such a way that every lived minute seemed to us like something irreducible. Therefore, in spite of ourselves, we came to this conclusion, which will seem shocking to lofty souls: Evil cannot be redeemed.

'But, on the other hand, most of the resisters, though beaten, burned, blinded, and broken, did not speak. They broke the circle of Evil and reaffirmed the human—for themselves, for us, and for their very torturers. They did it without witness, without help, without hope, often even without faith. For them it was not a matter of believing in man but of wanting to. Everything conspired to discourage them: so many indications everywhere about them, those faces bent over them, that misery within them. Everything concurred in making them believe that they were only insects, that man is the impossible dream of spies and squealers, and that they would awaken as vermin like everybody else.

'This man had to be invented with their martyrized flesh, with their hunted thoughts which were already betraying them—invented on the basis of nothing, for nothing, in absolute gratuitousness. For it is within the human that one can distinguish means and ends, values and preferences, but they were still at the creation of the world and they had only to decide in sovereign fashion whether there would be anything more than the reign of the animal within it. They remained silent and man was born of their silence. We knew that every moment of the day, in the four corners of Paris, man was a hundred times destroyed and reaffirmed. . . .

'Five years. We lived entranced and as we did not take our profession of writer lightly, this state of trance is still reflected in our writings. We have undertaken to create a literature of extreme situations. . . .

'Therefore, we are Jansenists because the age has made us such, and in so far as it has made us touch our limits I shall say that we are all metaphysical writers. . . . For metaphysics is not a sterile discussion about abstract notions which have nothing to do with experience. It is a living effort to embrace from within the human condition in its totality.

'Forced by circumstances to discover the pressure of history, as Torricelli discovered atmospheric pressure, and tossed by the cruelty of the time into that forlornness from where we can see our condition as man to the very limit, to the absurd, to the night of unknowingness, we have a task for which we may not be strong enough (this is not the first time that an age, for want of talents, has lacked its art and its philosophy). It is to create a literature which unites and reconciles the metaphysical absolute and the relativity of the historical fact. . . . It is not a question for us of escaping into the eternal or of abdicating in the face of what the unspeakable Mr. Zaslavsky calls in *Pravda* the "historical process".' (*What is Literature?* pp. 160–165.)

There is rhetoric in these extracts, but they are not rhetoric. As Hobbes's state of nature before the social contract is sometimes realized historically in the anarchy of national sovereign states, so in these extreme situations the source of civilization in the absolute will of the isolated individual was not merely a metaphysical myth. It is Kierkegaard's vision of political events forcing the individual back into his ethical isolation or dissipating him in the dust of nonentity. Again, it is Kierkegaard's figure of that sister of Destiny who cuts the thread when the quantitative individual decision has spread itself about and imposes itself as a new quality—an objective value. The individual in virtue of his human transcendence is a concrete universal. All I think, decide, and do separates me from the solid ground of what is there, and this is to universalize myself as man, to give man an essence by my existence—which is quite different from making myself a particular realization of a universal already given.

The relation of individual and universal is the central persistent theme of philosophical debate. The concrete historical universal of Hegel or the abstract rational universal of Kant owes nothing to personal decision. If the universal is once truly valid it does not need to be willed, it requires to be obeyed; the all-important thing is not the liberty of the individual in face of it, but the fertilization and development of the individual under its regime, not the assent of the person but the expansion and expense of the personality in its name. Therefore, it is frivolous to force the person to choose in ethical isolation, because what matters to him and to all is to bring him out on the right side, so that everything works out well. The answer of the existentialist is that man cannot be simply and finally brought under and identified with any law, whether it be promulgated as the law of his nature or as the law of the universe; the rule cannot justify the act nor the person, for only the act justifies the rule, as the paint not the school justifies the painter. In rejecting the view that personality gets whatever dignity and value it has from the universals which it adopts or to which it submits, existentialism does not hold that personality has a moral dignity or mystic value of its own which it communicates to whatever it adheres to; the rejection is based on an appreciation of the structure of personal being and universal being: man cannot be man and be bound, even by himself, and the world is open and cannot be circumvallated by universals and kept snug and safe. The individual act is always absolute and never final: this is the uncompromising theme of existentialist meditation. Of course the function of universals as information is not affected by the criticism of them as absolutes. Indeed, the point just is that they have their source in experience and not in the structure of man nor in the structure of the universe.

The violence and fantastic abstractness of some of Sartre's ethical pronouncements, then, must be read in the light of the extreme situations and radical issues of the present phase in human affairs. Even a theory founded upon a metaphysical absolute—the eternal situation of man—is not to be taken out of its context in the existing historical situation. Not the least virtue of this existentialist theory or affirmation at this time is the leaven of tolerance which it introduces. The liberty of all is implied by and is necessary to the liberty of each. The concern is to awaken each to his liberty, not to convert him to a doctrine. 'The very maximum of what one human being can do for another in relation to that wherein each man has to do solely with himself, is to inspire him with concern and unrest' (Kierkegaard). Communication is promoted and the poison of moralism eliminated. It is not the tolerance of easygoing indifference, for in rejecting the fanatical or intransigent either-or aimed at the life of the other it espouses the either-or within the self of personal decision and absolute responsibility. Thus it is an ethic of human solidarity, without crying peace, peace, where there is no peace—where there is the degradation of man to a thing.

In sum, then, existentialism is in contrast with other philosophies in its insistence on the ambiguity arising out of fundamental structural discontinuities. The characteristic attempt of philosophy to reduce the discontinuities is rejected, in evolutionary naturalism with its doctrine of emergence and refusal of reduction not less than in a monistic materialism or idealism. The discontinuities are existential and have to be lived, they are not problems for thought. The separation of man from the world and from himself is constitutive of his being and is the occasion of philosophy not the problem for philosophy. The discontinuity between thought and existence makes it vain to propose a solution within the unity of thought. The discontinuities are both preserved and modified in action; there is a practical nisus towards a concrete synthesis in the life of a person, of a university, of a culture: in this sense, and in this sense only, is there a concrete universal, but it does not precede action, is not binding on the future, and does not end in a total achievement.

A philosophy that is thus tolerant of discontinuities is not a philosophy of causal laws; it is a philosophy of essences. It is not concerned with explaining, nor changing, nor contemplating the world, but, rather, with lived participation in it.[1] A philosophy of essences is the theoretic attempt to isolate and explore independent ultimate structures and meanings: *pour-soi* and *en-soi* and *pour-autrui*, *Dasein* and *Zuhandene* and *Vorhandene* and *Sorge*, having and being and doing, instead, say, of biological propensities, reflex mechanisms, organic and inorganic, the division of our nature into cognitive, affective, and conative aspects. The intellectual reason for this phenomenological approach is a respect for things as they are in their regional totalities, a refusal of reductive analysis and of theoretical synthesis, a revision of the canons and assumptions of rationality. The practical reason is to use this appreciation of structures in 'a living effort to embrace from within the human condition in its totality'—in order to live it. Such a philosophy sets no goals. For nothing can be achieved once for all or objectively established for mankind; human existence is realized in personal being, and personal being is a difficult and precarious individual attainment constantly striven for and never permanently possessed, but upheld, drawn on, and rewarded by the

---

[1] Existentialism is not a baroque harmony wrought out of conflicts and strains, like the poetry of the seventeenth-century mystics, the cry for a God who is already possessed. Rather, it is in the modern manner of Paul Klee, the skilful practical management of several dimensions, discontinuities, based on profound appreciation of the structural relations of certain formal elements, beginning with an act of free choice developed by assimilation of random elements of experience into an object that is also a sign, a strange encounter expressive and exploratory. Compare, for example, Sartre's break with the spirit of seriousness which considers that bread is desirable because we *must* live and it *is* nourishing, instead of attending to the simple materiality of things knowing what one is about, for the sake of their symbolic value for the ideal project of man.

rich responsiveness of an objective world. Such a philosophy says little, too little (with the great exception of Jaspers), about history and science, or, it would be better to say, rejects historicism and scientism and exalts the historian and the scientist. When Ortega y Gasset says, 'Man has no nature, what he has is history', or Heidegger or Sartre says that with man existence precedes essence, they are not professing any form of historicism; they are agreeing with Hegel and Marx and Vico that man is only what he does, and has no substance or essence by which he can be intuitively and absolutely known and by which he is or should be determined. But they are not agreeing that he is historically determined. They are saying that in what he makes himself to be in his deeds the existing individual becomes an essence to others and to himself, but it is an essence which he can own or repudiate, to which he can react and by which he is not bound. This negative capability is a metaphysical absolute which constitutes man and is eternally true of him independent of historical change, although his proper concern with it can be entirely eclipsed by the historical social preoccupations of the age; it is not itself a positive essence since it has no content and does not determine him in any way but puts him in question, or, in the violent but pregnant phrase of some existentialists, makes it that he is nothing. He sees himself in his institutions and tasks and tools and techniques, and all that is objectively before him, but he separates himself from them even in order to maintain and work them. By separating himself he perpetually puts himself in question, and thereby puts also in question all that is there before him, all that is given as well as all that he has done and made. But the liberty of separation is always insistently conjoined with the facticity and historicity of the embodied self in a situation, bonds and limits are as much the theme as possibility and opportunity, commitment and fidelity as much as project and choice. Therefore it is neither a vain defiance of history and fate, nor an awakening to acceptance in common of the freedom of necessity; it is an awakening to acceptance in individual isolation of the necessity of freedom, the condition of a genuine *amor fati*.

Anything that offers to save man from the difficulties and dangers of this situation is merely one of the temptations which beset the pilgrim's path and lure him from the destiny of personal being. Man not only manifests himself in history by the deeds of all individual men known and unknown, but also fights in the individual for his authenticity against the great objectivities, the universals, abstract and concrete, which he has made, against the premature *rigor mortis* which creeps in from all quarters. The danger is not only from the devouring maw of the industrial machine, bureaucratic administration, and the totalitarian state; and from the banditry of militant ideologies with their incessant fire of propaganda, but also not less in the holy places of security, in science and morals and law, in Christianity and in humanism. Faith in science, or reason, or duty, or *homo faber*, or Christ, if it stands between the individual and his total responsibility hides him from himself. It is a hard doctrine, a challenge to everybody and to everything, a call to heroism: hence the strain and stress in existentialist writings, the anguish, the 'extreme situations'. Hence the exaggerations, and the derision it excites.

For it is easy, too easy, to satirize: it guys itself. Two sentences chopped out of *L'Être et le Néant*, like a decapitated cockerel running round in a circle, will provide sport for all any day of the week. But so will a man who says he is King of the Jews, and is provided with a crown of thorns. The times are too serious, the historical issues too fateful and tormenting to amuse oneself at the expense of too obviously ridiculous prophets. If one asks which side they are on in the present battle of ideologies, the answer can only be that, in spite of the striking personal differences in their own strong political and religious convictions and antipathies, their common thought agrees that to force the issue between ideologies on the plane of power is the most radical and ruinous falsification of the human situation that is possible. They stand for the restoration of the possibility of philosophy and the possibility of communication, for a multiplicity of approaches and a plurality of studies and activities and experiences, each defining its own guiding ideas, and not dependent upon a master philosophy nor supervised by a central authority. Whether any one of them has seriously enough faced the practical problems which are involved in such a view, that is, the problem of modern civilization itself, is perhaps a question. To take this philosophy either as a romantic pessimism or as a work of reactionary defence is the completest misunderstanding; it is essentially a work of salvage and salvation. But it excels in protest, challenge, warning, reminder, and is not an adequate constructive effort. One recalls Heidegger's mythological characterization of the age, following the poet Hölderlin, as a time of need because it lies under a double negation, the no-more of the gods that have fled and the not-yet of the god that is coming. It is false and futile to return, and even worse to take the future by storm. If one abandons the speculative heights and takes up a bold position on the face of the crag immediately above the normal human standpoint, it is possible really to get a view of the human situation *sub specie aeternitatis*, and that is the view which the times demand, when some are lost on the heights and most are scattered and stuck fast in things as they are in the valleys below.

An age which has discovered and recognized absolute evil, not in the heart of man but in the contemporary deeds of men, has to come to terms with itself, and that is what we find going on in the later development of existentialism, confirming its foundations. That is why it is a call to heroism and has so little to do with average hopes and fears and with the themes of an earlier humanism. If it proposes liberation by enlightenment, as did those earlier humanists, it does not mean, as they did, emancipation by scientific knowledge of the laws of the universe and of man and of society, but awakening to total individual responsibility—'I am my own witness'. If as a movement it stops short at this harsh conversion, it can hardly go further without going back on itself; and its individual exponents do go further in furnishing their own witness and representative example. Thus each of them makes his own contribution to the problem of civilization which confronts the modern world, and each of them must be left to his own singular fate and fortune in meeting criticism and carrying conviction in the professional controversies of the schools.

Even in these days, academic groves are cool and sequestered, and it is understandable that in such quarters a pulpit philosophy should be resented and deplored, for the new friars, more frothily corruptive of youth than ancient sophists, let loose an immense untidiness and with uncouth shouts set up their morality show and parade the hectic of disease and the scandal of sin against a backcloth of the vast and the vague. Nothing could be more annoying, more offensive to the taste of a chaste intellect. Except of course that it is fun to dispose of it by neat snips with the scissors of logic in a magazine article, or to dry it up in a lecture by judicious dabs of an astringent wit, or even to jolly well put it in its place by persistent snubs in reviews. When all is said, however, these six thinkers remain formidable persons, marvellously gifted, highly trained, masters of Western culture, with exceptional seriousness of purpose and a profound personal experience. One may not be convinced by the total philosophy of any one of them, but, odd as they are, they are representative, because they are trying not merely to think but personally to live the situation of man embedded in the situation of their time. They are profoundly in touch; whatever one makes of them, to have no use for them at all is to be profoundly out of touch. Their influence, whatever its effect, has not been slight. Kierkegaard has percolated into theology and is so thoroughly diffused that it is hardly possible to take up a current sample that does not show his trace. The impact of Sartre on the French theatre and novel, developing a literature of extreme situations rather than of character, and metaphysical rather than moral, has set more in motion than can yet be discerned. The great torrent of German metaphysics plunges into a fall with Heidegger and Jaspers that has certainly attracted attention. The themes and the temper of this thought have penetrated everywhere in the West, not without distortion, and a remarkable number of outstanding and influential minds have been decisively affected. The contemporary fact, then, is that these six thinkers are to be seen as exerting real power and as exciting real contempt. The time has not yet come to attempt a sober historical assessment; for it is still as a contribution to our own thought and action that we have to consider their work, in facing the decisions of our personal lives and the problem of our civilization.

BIOGRAPHICAL NOTES

KIERKEGAARD

Kierkegaard was born, lived, and died in Copenhagen, and left it only for two stays of several months in Berlin and one or two other short visits there and elsewhere. His father came from a desolate part of Jutland where as a child, one of nine, he struggled desperately with the grim conditions of his life until at the age of twelve he was taken by an uncle to Copenhagen to help him in his business. There the father made a fortune by trading, and retired at the age of forty after the death of his wife. Kierkegaard, born in 1813, was the last of seven children by a second marriage, to a distant relative living as a servant in the house. The father occupied his retirement with theological and philosophical study and discussion. He was profoundly melancholy and exerted a powerful and sombre influence upon Kierkegaard, communicating to the child his preoccupation with his own guilt and the most violent concepts of the Christian faith. Kierkegaard later described this treatment as 'spiritual rape'. Whilst Kierkegaard was at the university, his mother, a brother, and two sisters died, leaving as survivors of the family with himself only his father and eldest brother, who was intellectually gifted but morbidly religious and undermined by introspection. About this time Kierkegaard freed himself from the direct domination of his father (probably by guessing something of his guilty secrets) and gave himself up to the intellectual and social influences of student life. He fell in love with a girl of fourteen. Some three years after the break with his father, when Kierkegaard was twenty-five, they were reconciled, and his father died, leaving him the house and independent means. Out of loyalty to his father, he spent two years completing the theological studies which had become distasteful to him. He then became engaged to Regina, at that time seventeen. Within a year he broke with her because of internal scruples, pretending, in order to overcome her resistance, that he had been playing with her affections. He went to Berlin, eager to hear Schelling lecture on the Hegelian system, but was disappointed and soon returned. For the remaining fifteen years of his life he was engaged in the production of his works, more than twenty publications. When he had established a reputation with his first books, he got embroiled in a feud with the *Corsair*, a scurrilous but clever sheet, which for the best part of a year featured him as the butt of its ridicule and haunted his public appearances—there is evidence that he was a hunchback. This experience of persecution confirmed in him the serious bent of his authorship, which culminated some years later in a sustained and vehement attack upon the Established Church as neither Christian nor honest. He collapsed in the course of conducting this attack, and died after some six weeks in hospital in 1855 at the age of forty-two.

NIETZSCHE

Nietzsche was born in 1844, near Leipzig, son of a Protestant pastor, who died before the child was five. At school he was influenced by Greek studies and by the poet Hölderlin, himself a passionate Grecian. Meant for the Church, he abandoned theology for philology and followed Ritschl from the university of Bonn to that of Leipzig, where Goethe had been inscribed a student one hundred years earlier. He took Goethe as his master, fell under the spell of Schopenhauer, read the Greeks, above all the pre-Socratics, and such moderns as Novalis, Brentano, and Heine. During his period of military service an injury to the chest proved troublesome and he was invalided out. He finished his studies at Leipzig and obtained a chair in philology at Basel, where he was a colleague of Jacob Burckhardt. Before he left Leipzig he had met Wagner there, and at Basel he was within easy reach of their home and formed an enchanted intimacy with Wagner and Cosima: music had always been a necessity to him. In the next ten years, his health broke down and he became alienated by Wagner's romantic Germanism and mystical Christianity. He had to give up his post. During the following ten years, 1879–1889, without country, profession, or home, racked by *migraine*, and moving from place to place (with sometimes six or seven residences in a year), he wrote the books by which he is known. In the year 1889 mental disorder supervened, and he remained deranged till he died in 1900 at Weimar in the care of his sister.

JASPERS

Jaspers was born in 1883 at Oldenburg, the son of a bank manager. As a youth, he studied law at Heidelberg and Munich, before devoting himself during the next five years to the study of medicine, at Berlin, Göttingen, and Heidelberg. He worked as scientific assistant in the psychiatric clinic in Heidelberg before the first world war. He was appointed to the chair of philosophy at Heidelberg in 1921, after five years' teaching on the staff. He was dismissed for political reasons by the National-Socialist government in 1937, and reinstated in 1945. Since 1948 he has been professor of philosophy at Basel.

MARCEL

Marcel was born in 1889 into a cultivated family, his father being French Minister in Stockholm and afterwards director of one or another of the great national collections. His mother died when he was four, and he was brought up by an aunt. The image of his mother (a radiant personality) and the dominion of his aunt (an austere agnostic) maintained a tension of which he has said, 'this hidden polarity between the seen and the unseen has played a far greater part in my life and thought than any other influence which may be apparent in my writings'. From his childhood he had much opportunity of travel, and places played an important formative part in his development. During the first world war, he was not fit for active

167

service and was engaged for the Red Cross in tracing the missing, an experience which brought home to him the world of difference between the third person and the second. From youth he engaged in dramatic writing (he has published more than fifteen pieces) and in philosophical studies, beginning with the Idealism of German, English, and American thinkers. Musical composition and improvisation interest him so much that he has said, 'It was my true vocation, in that alone I am creative'. He has taught intermittently since 1912. He was baptised into the Roman Church in 1929 at the age of 39.

HEIDEGGER

Heidegger, born in 1889, belongs to the Black Forest region and is of a Catholic peasant family. He was actively interested from early youth in Western theology and philosophy. In 1915 he got a lectureship in philosophy at Freiburg, where he came under the influence of Husserl who was professor of philosophy there from 1916–29. Heidegger made a reputation as a stimulating and original teacher and was appointed to the chair of philosophy at Marburg in 1923, where he wrote *Sein und Zeit*, published in 1927. He returned to Freiburg to succeed Husserl in 1929. He was elected Rector in 1933 after Hitler came to power, and resigned the post early in the following year. His time is now mainly spent in the rude solitude of a ski-ing hut high up in the mountains of the Black Forest, with the cherished works of Hölderlin.

SARTRE

Sartre, born in 1905, studied at the École Normale Supérieure in Paris, and went to Havre to teach at the Lycée. Later he taught at the Lycée Henri IV before going to the Institut Français in Berlin in 1934. In the following year he joined the staff of the Lycée Condorcet, from which he resigned in 1942 to devote himself to his literary work. From 1939–41 he was in the army, and spent nine months as a prisoner of war in Germany. After his release, he was active in the resistance movement from 1941–44. Since its inception in 1945, he has edited the monthly review *Les Temps Modernes*.

BIBLIOGRAPHICAL NOTES

KIERKEGAARD

All the important works are now available in English, published in America by the Princeton University Press and in England by the Oxford University Press. Walter Lowrie, the chief translator, has done a short life (*A Short Life of Kierkegaard*) and a longer biographical and critical study (*Kierkegaard*). The same publishers have issued with the series of translations *A Kierkegaard Anthology*, edited by Robert Bretall, which gives representative selections from eighteen works, with explanatory introductions.

BIBLIOGRAPHICAL NOTES

NIETZSCHE

Complete works translated into English in eighteen volumes, edited by Oscar Levy, London and New York, 1909–13.

Nietzsche. By H. A. Reyburn. Macmillan, 1948. (A useful recent life.)

JASPERS

Man in the Modern Age. Translated by Eden and Cedar Paul. Kegan Paul, 1933. Revised edition 1952.

The Perennial Scope of Philosophy. Translated by Ralph Manheim. Kegan Paul, 1950. (Lectures delivered in the University of Basel since the war.)

The European Spirit. Translated, with an Introduction, by Gregor Smith. Student Christian Movement Press, 1948. (A paper given at the international meetings in Geneva, 1946.)

'Philosophy and Science.' (An article in *World Review*, March 1950.)

MARCEL

The Philosophy of Existence. Translated by Manya Harari. The Harvill Press, 1948. (Four essays; two defining his position and doctrine, one autobiographical, one a critique of Sartre.)

The Mystery of Being. Part I: Reflection and Mystery. Harvill Press, 1950. (The first instalment of Marcel's Gifford Lectures.)

Being and Having. Translated by Katherine Farrer. Dacre Press, 1950.

HEIDEGGER

Existence and Being. Vision Press, 1949. (A substantial part of the volume is given to an account of *Sein und Zeit* by Werner Brock, a former colleague of Heidegger's at Freiburg; and there are four carefully translated essays chosen by Heidegger for the purpose of this first presentation of his thought in English.)

SARTRE

Existentialism and Humanism. Translated, with an Introduction, by Philip Mairet. Methuen, 1950. (An exposition and defence of his views in a popular lecture, followed by discussion.)

Baudelaire. Translated by Martin Turnell. Horizon, 1949.

Portrait of the Anti-Semite. Translated by Erik de Mauny. Secker & Warburg, 1948.

What is Literature? Translated by Bernard Frechtman. Methuen, 1950.

The Psychology of the Imagination. Rider, 1951.

By Simone de Beauvoir. *The Ethics of Ambiguity.* Translated by Bernard Frechtman. Philosophical Library, New York, 1948.

Novels: *The Age of Reason*. Hamish Hamilton, 1946.
             The Reprieve. Hamish Hamilton, 1948.
             Iron in the Soul. Hamish Hamilton, 1950.
             The Chips are Down. Rider, 1951.

Theatre: *Three Plays*. John Lehmann, 1947.

Note.—None of the main philosophical works of the contemporary existentialist thinkers has been translated into English.

INDEX

(Semi-colons have been used to separate page references to different Thinkers under headings of the same doctrine.)

Absolute:
  choice, 15 ff.; 33; 49; 131
  engagement, 80
  meaning of existence, 100 ff.
  value, 113
  consciousness an, 111
  individual an, 57; 160
  man an, 162
  concrete meaning of, 77

Action:
  analysis of, 127 ff.
  as form of being or having, 81; 139

Being:
  access to, 56; 70, 73, 74; 105, 108; 141, 142
  cannot be thought, 7; 25; 45 ff.; 83; 103
  description of, 112
  discontinuities of, 9 ff.; 44, 58; 82
  not a problem, 69
  the object of philosophy, 58; 67; 87, 107
  as Transcendence, 62, 64

Body:
  and personal consciousness, 68, 71 ff, 81, 84; 117, 119 ff.

Choice:
  of self, 9, 15 ff.; 25, 26, 33; 48 ff.; 74 ff.; 96 ff.; 129 ff., 141
  Heidegger's treatment compared with Kierkegaard's, 107

Christianity:
  permanently disconcerting, 5
  the kernel of, 29

  its modern form, 34
  its persistence, 35, 39

Conflict:
  inescapable, 53; 126

Conscience:
  Nietzsche's conception of, 26, 27
  Heidegger's conception of, 97, 99

Death:
  as situational limit, 52
  as sovereign possibility of personal existence, 95 ff.
  as task of life, 107
  as a mere fact, 135, 136

Despair:
  source of, 16; 52; (as dread) 94, 95, 104; 113, 142
  an option, 41; 62; 70, 71, 78, 81

Essence:
  existence precedes, 128; 162
  of man, 49, 51; 151, 162

Existence (*see also* Choice):
  personal, structure of, 88 ff.; 112 ff.; 151
  — authentic, 8 ff., 18 ff.; 23, 33, 37, 40; 48 ff., 59; 71 ff., 74 ff.; 92, 96, 98; 132 ff., 147; 162
  — an experience of reality, 56 ff.; 78, 80, 84; 104 ff.; 147, 148
  impersonal, 13, 20 21; 38; 57; 81; 91; 133

Existentialism:
  a protest against Hegel, 2, 7
  a standpoint within existence, 8, 20; 25; 83; 103

a recall of philosophy to the concrete, 3, 7 ff., 15 ff.; 23, 36; 44, 48; 67, 68, 70; 89, 98
a philosophy of Being, 149

Existentialism—*continued*.
a philosophy of essences, 161
a philosophy of synthesis in personal existence, 10 ff; 37, 38; 44, 47, 48, 58, 63, 64; 83; 99 ff.; 132 ff.; 153, 161
a philosophy of tolerance, 160, 163
a philosophy of salvation, 163

Faith:
irreconcilable with reason, 3 ff.
object of, 14 ff.
philosophical, 56 ff., 61 ff.
justification of, 78 ff., 84

Fate:
amor fati, 33, 35; 55, 62, 63; (72); 96; (137, 146); 162
facticity, 52 ff.; 97, 99; 113, 131 ff.

God:
not the world nor other than the world, 59
not a third party, 20; 79
as a third party, 125
is not-yet, 103
man's desire to be, 138
a contradiction, 113, 142

Guilt:
Jasper's conception of, 54
Heidegger's conception of, 97, 99
Sartre's conception of, 123

Having:
and being, 70 ff.; 140 ff.
and knowing, 127
and doing, 139 ff.
and disposability, 80 ff.

Hegel:
Kierkegaard's opposition to, 2, 7
on Judaism, 6 n.
his ethical philosophy, 19
his thesis, 150

Heidegger:
not an existentialist, 86
an existentialist, 108
compared with Jaspers, 106

Husserl:
and existentialism, 87

Individual:
nineteenth century contempt for, 13
ethical isolation and responsibility of, 8, 15, 17, 21, 22; 31, 37, 40, 41; 48, 51, 57, 61; 92, 94; 137; 154 ff, 162, 164

Jaspers:
his study of Kierkegaard and Nietzsche, 43
his doctrine of ciphers, 60 ff.
his achievement, 64
compared with Heidegger, 106

Kierkegaard:
a solitary, 1
psychological roots of his philosophy, 2, 18
his early study of Hegel, 2
his criticism of Kant and Hegel, 7
his criticism of the age, 13, 15, 16, 17, 34
his individualism, 21
his subjectivism, 16, 18n., 22
his mission, 6, 22
compared with Nietzsche, 23

Language:
existential root of, 93
degradation of, 94
has an outside, 121
has an inside, 133

Liberty:
human existence is, 48, 59; 128, 129
and law, 51; 76; 159
its limits, 52 ff.; 134 ff.
the primary subject-object relation 71, 74

Marcel:
home influence on his thought, 77
his method, 66
a Christian humanist, 72, 78
his criticism of Idealism, 68
his doctrine of mystery, 69, 83
his doctrine of fidelity, 74 ff.
his strength and weakness, 85

Negation:
as withdrawal, 16; 94; 111 ff.

Negation—*continued*.
  as affirmation, 33, 35; 96, 100
  as frustration, 52, 61 ff.; 113,
    123 ff., 142
  interpretation of, 104 ff., 108; 147
Nietzsche:
  psychological roots of his philo-
    sophy, 24
  his purpose, 24, 30, 36, 39
  his criticism of the age, 28, 33, 34
  his achievement, 41
  not a scientific materialist, 31
  retained Schopenhauer's meta-
    physics, 26, 33
  his understanding of Kierkegaard,
    38
  Jaspers's criticism of, 62
  compared with Kierkegaard, 23, 36,
    40

Object:
  of faith, 14 ff.
  of thought, 6 ff.; 24 ff.; 45; 67 ff.;
    114 ff.
  of experience, 56; 68 ff., 73, 74, 83;
    111
  primary, 71
  ultimate, 74
  as tool, 89
  as given, 90
  as person, 9; 57; 76, 79 ff.; 117 ff.
  not situated in but constituted by
    time and space, 89, 90, 99

Objectivity:
  true, 37, 38
  pretentions of, 20; 45 ff., 56; 69 ff.
  the fight against, 3, 5, 13, 15, 20, 21;
    25, 33, 34; 53 ff., 57; 70, 71 ff.;
    91, 104, 105; 117 ff., 131 ff.; 159,
    162, 163

Philosophy:
  its source, 22, 150

Sartre:
  meets the charge of pessimism, 143

Sartre—*continued*.
  justifies his preoccupation with
    extremes, 155 ff.
  a rationalist, 146
  why not a marxist, 156
Science:
  Kierkegaard's criticism of, 10 ff., 15,
    16
  Nietzsche's criticism of, 28 ff.
  Jasper's criticism of, 45 ff.
  Marcel's criticism of, 67, 70, 77,
    83
  Heidegger's criticism of, 90, 104, 105
Subject:
  making of a, 9, 15, 21; 24, 26, 37;
    48; 67, 74; 88, 98; 113
  relation of subject to, 9; 57; 76, 79,
    83; 91; 117 ff.

Tension:
  of reason and faith, 4, 17, 18
  of ideals, 35
  of frustration, 52; 113, 123, 142
  of reason and experience, 69
  of being and having, 73; 141
  of personalities, 74
  of faith and despair, 61; 82
  of acceptance and refusal, 5; 96, 105
  of consciousness and the world, 113,
    147
  existential and irresolvable, 151 ff.,
    160
Truth:
  unattainable and useless, 25
  a christian ideal, 29
  personal, 16; 37; 57
  human, 90, 92 ff., 101 ff.; 114 ff.

Value
  genesis of, 26 ff.
  problem of, 31 ff.
  conflict of, 35, 40
  individual responsibility for, 11; 31,
    41; 51; 102; 131; 155 ff.
  absolute, 113